MUM'S not COOKiNG!

FAVOURITE SINGAPOREAN RECIPES FOR THE NEAR CLUELESS OR PLAIN LAZY

DENISE FLETCHER

EPIGRAM BOOKS / SINGAPORE

Cover design by Stefany
Illustrations by Kuan Teck Harn
Author's photograph by Sofjan S.

National Library Board, Singapore
Cataloguing-in-Publication Data

Fletcher, Denise, 1967-
Mum's not cooking : favourite Singaporean recipes
for the near clueless or plain lazy / Denise Fletcher.
– Singapore : Epigram Books, 2012.
p. cm.
Includes index.
ISBN : 978-981-08-9732-1 (pbk.)

1. Cooking, Singaporean. 2. Quick and easy cooking. I. Title.

TX724.5.S55
641.595957 -- dc22   OCN745851647

First Edition
10 9 8 7 6 5 4 3 2 1

CONTENTS

DEDICATED TO:

My three boys,

my mother,

Every mother, and every child,

Linda,

LQ—my tiny Canuck,

Alikatt, Laz, Cameron and

Nadia.

INTRODUCTION

As a mother of three boys, I understand the anxiety of letting go and watching from a distance. We think our children cannot get by without our care. It matters not, whether that child is seven or twenty-two. Our child remains our child and in our minds, helpless, even when they tower over us.

I remember as a newlywed, finding myself suddenly thrust into the role of keeper of all things and provider of nourishment for my husband, I was overwhelmed and didn't know where to begin! Vacuuming and laundry was one thing; putting entire meals on the table for my husband, whose culinary expectations I was just beginning to grasp, was another. I kept calling my mum at all and sometimes odd hours, asking how to select this ingredient or how to cook that dish. Bless her patience!

Spurred by these experiences, I wrote this book to allay the fears of parents, inspire confidence in students about to leave home and country and dive into independence, and guide newlyweds (or anyone else!) who want to cook our beloved local dishes, but haven't a clue where to begin.

It's an exciting time, but it can also be a fearful one. Whatever you do, you'll need to eat, so the recipes here are simple and clear, the ingredients easy to find and the results dependably delicious and, where possible, healthy. Many local favourites are here, simplified, so you can focus on the important stuff—your books, your future, your budding career, your shiny new marriage! If you start to miss home or mum's cooking, I hope you will find a dependable resource and a fount of comfort, between the covers of this book.

Cooking, while often viewed as a lesser ability, is peerless in inspiring confidence, developing organisation, management and budgeting skills, and encouraging creativity and imagination. The ability to cook means you will be surrounded by friends, willing dish washers, and, you will never go hungry. The love for cooking will provide an invaluable outlet for busting stress, something that, unfortunately at this juncture, you will know only too well. Sure, there's always pizza delivery, McDonald's or Chinese take-out. But, seriously, how much pizza or take-out can you eat?

I hope this book will become your kitchen companion and a voice that reassures you as your mother might, when you have questions and doubts. Good luck on your journey of learning and living, and one last thing; don't forget to eat something every now and then!

DENISE FLETCHER

KITCHEN 101

The kitchen can be an overwhelming and dangerous place. Know your paring knife from your peeler and navigate your way safely around the cooking hob and cutting board, so you will never need to worry if you're doing things right, or who's going to drive you to the A&E.

USING THIS BOOK

CUP measurements in this book refer to the standard 200 ml capacity (filled to the brim) tea cup found in most kitchens.

TSP measurements refer to the standard 5 ml teaspoon used in most kitchens for stirring sugar into your coffee or tea.

TBSP measurements refer to the standard 15 ml tablespoon used to eat your dinner with. These spoons are larger than conventional soup spoons.

Unless otherwise stated, all measurements are level.

LIGHT VEGETABLE OIL refers to any neutral tasting and smelling vegetable cooking oil like soy, sunflower seed, grape seed, canola or corn oil. Corn oil is slightly heavier in texture than the other oils mentioned. Olive oil (especially virgin and extra virgin olive oil), sesame oil and flavoured oils are primarily used as flavour accents and are not all-purpose cooking oils.

OVEN TEMPERATURES AND TIMES given work well for my own oven. All ovens differ to a degree and you may find it necessary to adjust the given times and/ or temperatures for your own oven.

MICROWAVE-SAFE DISHES AND TRAYS refer to non-metallic, silicone, plastic, glass, ceramic, stoneware or pottery ones that are marked "microwave-safe" by the manufacturer. Metal receptacles or receptacles with metallic paint decorations should never be used in the microwave oven as they create sparks, which can cause a fire in the microwave oven and short circuit it. While most plastics won't melt in the microwave, you should still only use microwave-safe plastic containers as these have been made from food grade plastics that won't leak out harmful chemicals into your food when they reach high temperatures.

OVEN PROOF DISHES AND TRAYS refer to metal or silicone, ceramic, glass, stoneware and pottery ones that are marked "ovenproof" by the manufacturer. This indication can usually be found on the base of the dish or tray. These are specifically manufactured to withstand the high temperatures required in baking, roasting and oven grilling.

KITTING OUT YOUR KITCHEN

THE BASICS

I don't expect that you will be rushing out to completely re-kit your kitchen or get specialist gadgets and equipment. Neither do I think that you should. It's perfectly possible to cook effectively, economically, easily and enjoyably with a little improvisation and imagination. The following are suggestions for items I find useful in the kitchen, but feel free to get as many or as few as you feel necessary or to add your own favourites.

GENERAL

- Medium-sized Chinese wok (well seasoned cast iron or non-stick, preferably round bottomed)
- Small- to medium-sized frying pan (you should be able to fry two eggs in it at once)
- Small- to medium-sized deep lidded pot
- Very tall lidded pot (for boiling pasta and blanching noodles)
- Ladle
- Fryer
- Noodle blancher
- Medium-sized steel mixing bowl
- Large-sized steel mixing bowl

- Easy to read kitchen scale (clearly marked in 10 g or 20 g graduations)
- Medium-sized handheld balloon whisk
- Medium-sized chef's knife (with a 20 cm long blade for almost any cutting/peeling/chopping job in the kitchen as its slightly curved blade edge makes it a very comfortable, versatile and efficient tool, unlike most other knives which are made for specific jobs)
- Paring knife (for cutting/peeling fruit and small items of food)
- Medium-sized chopper (parang)
- Easy to use knife sharpener
- Easy to use can/bottle cap opener
- Easy to use vegetable peeler with stainless steel movable blade (for peeling fruits and vegetables that are too awkwardly shaped for the paring knife)
- Medium-sized chopping board (for fruit, bread and ready to eat foods that require no further cooking)
- Large-sized chopping board (for raw meat, vegetables and other foods that require further cooking)
- Multi-use grater
- Kitchen paper

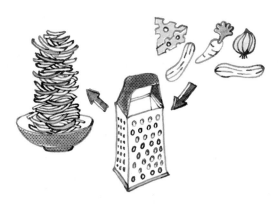

BAKING

- Medium-sized round cake tin (23 cm)
- Baking tray or swiss roll pan
- A 6-cup muffin tray or a 12-cup muffin tray (if you really, really like muffins)
- Muffin tray liners/cases
- Baking or parchment paper
- Easy to read kitchen scale (see above)
- A large rectangular steel or wire cooling rack
- Mixing bowls (see above)
- Hand whisk (see above)

APPLIANCES

- Stick or immersion blender
- Small microwave oven
- Tabletop oven or toaster oven with temperature control
- Small rice cooker
- Electric or gas cooking range or a 2-burner electric hot plate

FRESHNESS IS EVERYTHING

There are times when you will find yourself reaching for a can or package of convenience, processed or instant food because you're tired, lazy or just out of ideas. Nothing wrong with that as long as you try to eat fresh as often as possible for your health's sake. When buying fresh food, which usually costs more than frozen or processed, make sure you get your money's worth by knowing how to select the best.

CHICKEN – look for firm, pale pink flesh that's free from unpleasant odours. A light film of moisture on the flesh indicates freshness, but sticky slime means it's past its prime.

PORK – look for loose grained, slightly moist and deep pink flesh that's free from unpleasant odours or sticky slime. Any fat present should be a creamy white colour. Avoid meat that looks wet (especially if you wish to fry, oven roast or grill) as it will continue to ooze liquid during cooking and will not brown well.

BEEF – look for loose grained and brownish red meat that smells pleasantly "beefy" and looks relatively dry on the surface, without any slime. Any fat present should be a very pale, yellowish white. Avoid tight grained meat (will be tough after cooking) or very bright red meat that looks wet and bloody (full of moisture and will shrink dramatically on cooking).

WHITE FLESHED FISH – look for firm flesh that is not too springy or rubbery (will toughen on cooking) and smells pleasantly of the sea but not obviously fishy. Bright, glassy and bulging eyes, and a light coating of slippery slime on whole fish mean it's fresh but this slime should never feel sticky or smell bad as this indicates staleness. When buying cut fillets or steaks, make sure the flesh is moist, smells pleasant, firm (but not too springy) with no slime or drying/curling/darkening edges. With fish steaks, the blood visible in the core of the central bone should be liquid and bright red, not dehydrated and brown.

OILY FISH – like salmon, mackerel or tuna will have darker coloured flesh which tends to be firmer with a more tightly packed grain. All other qualities that you look for in white fish will also apply here.

PRAWNS – look for firm fleshed, glistening prawns with firmly attached heads and round, protuberant eyes. For flavour and texture, fresh unpeeled prawns are best. This is not always possible though, especially in the West where ready-peeled frozen (often cooked) prawns are preferred as they are more convenient and less fiddly. Use whichever you prefer or whichever is readily available to you.

GREEN VEGETABLES – whether leafy or otherwise, these should be firm, vibrantly green and crisp. Avoid yellowed and wilted leaves or stems and those with too many obvious blemishes or parasites. On the other hand, vegetables that look absolutely perfect and blemish free may indicate liberal use of chemical pesticides, so choose and prepare wisely.

NON-GREEN OR COLOURED VEGETABLES – like white or red cabbage, brinjal (eggplant), squash, corn, tomatoes and peppers should be firm, crisp and brightly coloured. All other qualities you would look for in green vegetables would apply here too.

THIN SKINNED AND SOFT FRUIT – like apples, oranges, bananas, avocados, grapes, persimmons, berries, mangoes, etc., should feel evenly tender (but not soft) to the touch with no hard or extra soft spots. Skins should be tight, unbroken, evenly coloured and with little or no blemishes. Usually, these fruits (except for avocados) give off a rich and sweet fragrance when they are fully ripe.

THICK SKINNED FRUIT – like melons, durians, pineapples, etc., should feel heavy and have no soft spots (these indicate internal decay) or breaks/cracks. Pineapples, melons (all but the watermelon) and durians give off a strong scent (pleasant in the pineapple and melon, much less so in the durian) when ripe. Pineapples and durians have skins that darken on ripening, but melon skins generally remain the same colour ripe or unripe.

xiv MUM'S NOT COOKING

FOOD HANDLING AND HYGIENE

Always wash your hands thoroughly with soap when you return from the market or supermarket, before you handle any food and after handling raw food or meat.

Keep all kitchen surfaces and equipment clean.

Keep all kitchen rags, dishcloths, napkins and dish sponges clean and as dry as possible to prevent bacterial growth.

Avoid cross contamination by using different knives, utensils and cutting boards for raw and cooked food, whether preparing, cooking or eating, as in when dining on steamboat, hotplate tabletop grilling or hotpot.

SAFE FOOD STORAGE AND CONSUMPTION

Cool leftovers completely and quickly before storing in clean, securely covered containers in the fridge. Eat leftovers after reheating thoroughly and consume within 3 days.

Don't store cooked leftovers next or close to covered or uncovered raw meat, seafood, unwashed vegetables, eggs, etc., as cross contamination may occur.

Keep different food types e.g., dairy, meat, vegetables, fruit, in separate compartments in the fridge and ensure that no cross contamination occurs via contact or leaking/dripping liquids.

Avoid eating foods containing mayonnaise or dairy that have

remained unrefrigerated for more than an hour, especially in warm weather.

Wash fruit thoroughly before eating. Wash the inedible skin on fruit like melons, mangoes, papayas and pineapples thoroughly before cutting. The skins often harbour bacteria because of handling and if not washed off, can be easily transferred to the flesh of the fruit once cut open.

SAFE THAWING OF FROZEN FOOD

Thaw food quickly by using a microwave oven or gradually by storing overnight or over several days (for larger portions of food) in the meat chiller section of the fridge. Once thawed, cook immediately and completely.

You may safely thaw frozen food in cold water but ensure that the food is very securely packaged/wrapped to prevent water seepage, and change the water at close intervals until the food is completely thawed right through. Once thawed, cook immediately and completely.

Never thaw food out on the kitchen counter or anywhere else, at room temperature. Such conditions are ideal for present and dormant bacteria to come back to life and start multiplying.

Never refreeze thawed food, unless it has been thoroughly cooked after thawing.

KITCHEN SAFETY

Your mum probably doesn't want to read this bit, but it needs saying—

don't drink and drive, don't drink and cook. The kitchen can be a hot, steamy, slippery place with knives, hot surfaces and lots of furiously boiling liquids. If you haven't got it together, stay away and get take-out.

Keep the floor dry and grease-free; wipe up spills and clean up broken glass or crockery immediately.

If you have a gas tank or canister in the kitchen, make sure it's not leaking and that it's properly connected to the cooker.

Keep your knives sharp; you're much less likely to get nasty cuts if they're sharp and slice through foods easily.

When frying or deep-frying food, take care to thoroughly drain them as any water or excessive moisture present will cause the oil to spatter on contact with the water (sometimes quite explosively) and may cause injury to the hands, face or body.

When using a stick/immersion blender, make sure the blade is completely submerged in the liquid/food, before you turn it on, so you don't splash yourself with hot liquid.

If you have any doubts about the freshness or quality of any food, throw it away.

One last thing; please, please read the recipes once through from start to finish before attempting to do anything. Oh come on! They're so short! This one simple step may save you from accidentally missing out essential steps or ingredients and wrecking what could have been a great dish or meal! Boo hoo.

FRIDGE AND PANTRY LIST

The following list is ideal if you plan on fixing your own meals on a regular basis, but few things in life are ideal, so just try your best, or just get what you really like.

IN YOUR FRIDGE
GENERAL
- Bacon
- Ham
- Eggs

DAIRY
- Milk
- Dairy cream (made from cow's milk)
- Plain yoghurt
- Butter
- Cheese (Parmesan, mozzarella, Cheddar or your personal favourites)

SEASONINGS AND CONDIMENTS
- Prepared mustard (mustard in a yellow squeeze bottle)
- Ketchup
- Wasabi paste
- Tau cheo (fermented soy bean paste) or Miso paste

HERBS, SPICES FRUIT AND VEGETABLES
- Chillies (red/green/bird's eye—use these tiny but fiery chillies sparingly in your food/cooking as they are hot enough to peel the skin off your tongue. Don't touch your nose or eyes after handling them or you'll be very sorry!)
- Coriander leaves (cilantro)
- Spring onions
- Ginger
- Lemons
- Limes
- Lemongrass
- Pandan leaves (screwpine)
- Tomatoes
- Dried fruit (currants, golden or regular raisins, cranberries and apricots)
- A selection of your favourite fresh fruit

FREEZER
- Green peas
- Crumbed whole fish fillets
- Shelled prawns
- French fries
- Pizza bases
- Ice cream (did you think I'd forget?)

IN YOUR PANTRY
OIL
- All-purpose light vegetable cooking oil (soy, corn, canola, sunflower, etc.)
- Fragrant sesame oil
- Pure olive oil
- Extra virgin olive oil

FLAVOURINGS AND SEASONINGS
- Canned/packaged coconut milk (thick and thin)
- Oyster sauce
- Light soy sauce

- Dark soy sauce
- Sesame seeds (black or white)
- Thai fish sauce
- Thai tom yum paste
- White vinegar
- Granulated instant stock
- Garlic salt or garlic powder
- Prepared chilli paste or Korean gochujang
- Prepared garlic paste
- Prepared ginger paste
- Salted black beans (whole or paste)

DRIED HERBS AND SPICES
- Black pepper
- White pepper
- Chilli flakes
- Cinnamon (sticks and powder)
- Cardamom pods
- Whole cloves
- Cumin seeds
- Onions
- Garlic
- Dried oregano or marjoram, or mixed Italian herbs

STARCHES
- Dried spaghetti or your favourite long pasta variety
- Dried penne rigate or your favourite short pasta variety
- Basmati rice
- Thai fragrant rice or Jasmine rice
- Instant couscous
- Rolled oats
- Split red lentils

CANNED AND INSTANT FOOD
- Sardines
- Tuna
- Corned beef

- Cooked chickpeas
- Baked beans
- Pork luncheon meat
- Tomatoes (whole, diced, sliced, sauce, puree or paste)
- Ready fried crisp shallots (available at supermarkets)
- Instant mashed potatoes (flakes preferred over granules)
- Instant gravy mix (for mashed potatoes)
- Instant pancake mix

BAKING AND MISCELLANEOUS
- Baking soda (straight sodium bicarbonate—very versatile as a raising agent, cleaner for stubborn stains on pots and kitchen surfaces and effective fridge deodoriser. If using as a raising agent to make cake batter rise, it works best combined with double the amount of cream of tartar or appropriate amounts of other acidic agents like vinegar, citrus juice or yoghurt)
- Baking powder (usually a mixture of one part baking soda and two parts cream of tartar with a small amount of starch as a filler and trace amounts of aluminium compounds)
- Cream of tartar (used on its own to stabilise egg whites and increase volume when beating, and used in combination with baking soda as a raising agent)
- Dark chocolate chips
- Plain (all-purpose) flour
- Pure cocoa powder
- Pure good quality instant coffee granules
- Vanilla extract or essence
- Pandan essence or flavour
- Almonds or your favourite nuts
- Castor/superfine sugar
- Fine salt

BEEF, CHICKEN...OR FISH?

The recipes in this book all stand alone well enough, except of course for the side dishes, which are meant to be eaten with rice or other dishes. But, we all want to get a little fancy sometimes, toss things up or take it up a notch. These suggestions are meant to inspire or help if you're stuck for ideas, but as always, feel free to abbreviate, expand or completely ignore me—like you do your mum, and come up with your own combinations.

SEAFOOD
Assam Fish Curry 30
Prawn Omelette 31
Easy Cucumber and Pineapple Achar 67
White Rice 100

Steamed Fish with Ginger,
    Spring Onion and Soy Sauce 32
Savoury Steamed Eggs with Pork 53
Stir-fried Asian Greens 68
White Rice 100 or Cantonese Style
    Plain Rice Porridge 99

Black Pepper and Onion Tuna 34
Sambal Kang Kong 64
White Rice 100
Bubur Manis 108 or Sweet Potato in
    Ginger Syrup 122

Prawn Sambal 35
Sayur Lodeh 63 or Easy Cucumber and
    Pineapple Achar 67
Nasi Lemak 93 or White Rice 100

MEAT AND CHICKEN
Simple Beef Rendang 55 or Baked
    Crispy, Spicy Chicken Wings 50
Sambal Kang Kong 64 or Easy
    Cucumber and Pineapple Achar 67
Nasi Lemak 93 or White Rice 100

Easy Southeast Asian Chicken Curry 47
Sambal Kang Kong 64
Simple Tahu Goreng 62
White Rice 100

Fragrant Pork Balls with Napa
    Cabbage 46
Hot and Sour Szechuan Soup 26
Stir-fried Bitter Gourd with Salted Black
    Beans and Eggs 66
White Rice 100

Quick Curry Devil 49
Lobah 17
White Rice 100
Sugar Cane and Lime Jellies 117

VEGETARIAN
Spicy Chickpeas and Tomatoes 65
Indian Style Spinach Stir-fry 61
Easy Cucumber and Pineapple Achar 67
White Basmati Rice 100

Macaroni and Cheese 78
Garlic Bread 16
No Pastry Fruit Pie 118

Chap Chye (cooked without shrimps) 60
Stir-fried Bitter Gourd with Salted
    Black Beans and Eggs (omit eggs to
    make it vegan) 66
White Rice 100
Sweet Potato in Ginger Syrup 122

MIXED
Easy Fish Otah 33
Simple Beef Rendang 55
Easy Cucumber and Pineapple Achar 67
White Rice 100

Prawn Noodle Soup 84
Lobah 17
Brown Sugar and Coconut Agar-agar 113

Baked Crispy, Spicy Chicken Wings 50
Stir-fried Asian Greens 68 or Easy
    Cucumber and Pineapple Achar 67
Char Mee 80
Sugar Cane and Lime Jellies 117 or
    Sweet Potato in Ginger Syrup 122

No Roast Char Siew 45
Prawn Omelette 31
Stir-fried Asian Greens 68 or Easy
    Cucumber and Pineapple Achar 67
White Rice 100

Sardine and Tomato Curry 36
Baked Crispy, Spicy Chicken Wings 50
Indian Style Spinach Stir-fry 61
White Rice 100

Black Pepper and Onion Tuna 34
Baked Crispy, Spicy Chicken Wings 50
Instant Mash and Gravy
No Pastry Fruit Pie 118

WESTERN
Quick Cottage Pie 48
Your Favourite Green Salad
Chocolate Chip Mug Cake 112

Simple, Perfect Steak 52
Your Favourite Green Salad
French Fries
Black and White No-Bake
    Cheesecake 105

AFTERNOON TEA
Black Pepper and Onion Tuna
    Sandwiches 34
Polka Dot Slices 119
Jam Rolls 111 or Double Peanut
    Cookies 114
Coffee or Tea

Chinese Pumpkin Cake 10
Char Mee 80
Sugar Cane and Lime Jellies 117
Coffee, Tea or Chinese Tea

BREAKFAST AND SNACKS

BREAKFAST BANANA MUFFINS

BREAKFAST PIZZA

LAZY HAM AND EGG BREAKFAST

SOY SAUCE AND PEPPER FRIED EGGS

CORNED BEEF AND EGG BREAKFAST HASH

CHAI TOW KWAY

ROTI JOHN

CHINESE PUMPKIN CAKE

GERAGOK FRITTERS

SIMPLIFIED YEW CHAR KWAY

CURRY PUFFS

GARLIC BREAD

LOBAH

BREAKFAST BANANA MUFFINS

Prep 15 mins | Cook 20 mins | Makes 10 small muffins

The secret to fluffy, featherlight muffins is to mix or stir the ingredients with the absolute minimum number of strokes. Follow the instructions implicitly and you will be rewarded with moist, tender and fragrant muffins, so light, they might float out the window on a windy day!

150 G (1½ LOOSELY PACKED CUPS) PLAIN FLOUR

100 G (⅔ LOOSELY PACKED CUP) CASTOR SUGAR

1 TSP BAKING SODA

70 ML (⅓ CUP) LIGHT VEGETABLE OIL

130 ML (⅔ CUP) BUTTERMILK OR

THIN UNSWEETENED PLAIN YOGHURT

1 TSP VANILLA EXTRACT

1 LARGE VERY RIPE CAVENDISH BANANA,

FINELY MASHED WITH A FORK

1. Preheat the oven at 185°C. Line the muffin tray with muffin paper cases.

2. In a large, dry bowl, whisk together the flour, sugar and baking soda.

3. Make a well in the centre of the flour and add the oil, buttermilk, vanilla extract and banana.

4. Quickly and lightly give a few stirs with the whisk. **Do not over mix**.

5. Put one generous ice cream scoop of batter in each of the muffin cases and bake for 20 minutes or until well risen and golden and your kitchen smells delicious.

6. Serve warm with coffee, tea or milk.

Cavendish bananas are the most commonly found bananas in supermarkets. They tend to be large with thick peels, have sweet mild flesh and a relatively mild banana fragrance. The most prevalent brand is Del Monte.

If you use regular milk instead of buttermilk or yoghurt, you will not get the same light texture as baking soda works best to aerate and lighten the batter by reacting with the acids in buttermilk or yoghurt. If you cannot get buttermilk or yoghurt, add 1½ tablespoons of white or cider vinegar to an equivalent amount of regular milk.

To make a vegan version, substitute milk with water, rice milk, oat milk or soy milk soured with 1½ tablespoons of vinegar.

The soured milk or liquid can also be replaced with 2 teaspoons of cream of tartar added to the flour along with the baking soda. In which case, use milk of your choice or water for the liquid in the recipe.

BREAKFAST PIZZA

Prep 10 mins | Cook 15 mins | Serves 1

Mornings can be brutal; mental exhaustion and sleep deprivation don't make it easier. Few can face the prospect of a hot, freshly cooked breakfast, if there's no one to cook for you and when getting out of bed already feels like a task. Still, you'll need to get something substantial in your belly to kick start your gears for the long day ahead. Having frozen pizza bases and a few other kitchen essentials on hand means you'll never be out of eating options, especially when you're rushed, ravenous or just too knackered to do anything but the bare basics in the kitchen.

1 SMALL FROZEN PIZZA BASE (STRAIGHT FROM
   THE FREEZER)
2 RASHERS BACON, SLICED OR CUT WITH
   SCISSORS ANY WAY YOU WISH
1 EGG
AS MUCH GRATED CHEESE AS YOU LIKE
   (PARMESAN, MOZZARELLA OR A MIXTURE
   OF BOTH)
PINCH OF SALT
PINCH OF PEPPER

1. Preheat the oven at 190°C. If using a pizza toaster or toaster oven, preheat by turning the timer knob to 30 minutes position and put the dish in when the timer reaches 20 minutes.

2. Put the pizza base on an ovenproof plate. Top evenly with bacon slices and break the egg over the entre of the base.

3. Season with salt and pepper, scatter the cheese over and carefully transfer to the oven, ensuring that the egg doesn't spill over the edge.

4. Bake for 15 − 20 minutes or until the base is golden and crisp, the egg is done to your liking and the cheese is melted and golden.

5. Remove from oven and serve immediately. Take care when eating as the plate will be extremely hot.

My suggested toppings are what I feel would be easiest for days when you're rushed or exhausted. Feel free to use whatever else you prefer or have in your kitchen. (Examples are tomato slices, cheese slices, sausages, leftover shredded roast chicken, leftover curried meat, canned tuna, cooked spicy beans, peas, lentils, etc.)

LAZY HAM AND EGG BREAKFAST

Prep 5 mins | Cook 15 mins | Serves 1

I can't think of any breakfast easier than this, and I am a pretty lazy cook, always on the lookout for a quick and easy way out. You can vary the additions to the eggs. Try snipped bacon, diced tomato or cubed cheese. The important thing is to coat the inside of the dish really well with butter, for flavour, so you don't end up wasting your precious few minutes in the morning, wrestling the stuck eggs out of the dish.

A GENEROUS TBSP VERY SOFT BUTTER
1 LARGE SLICE HAM, DICED OR JUST RIPPED
    WITH YOUR FINGERS
1 SLICE BREAD, DICED OR JUST RIPPED
    WITH YOUR FINGERS
2 LARGE EGGS
PINCH OF SALT
PINCH OF PEPPER

1. Preheat the oven at 200°C.

2. Generously butter the inside of a small oval or rectangular baking dish.

3. Scatter the ham and bread evenly over the base.

4. Break the eggs over the ham and bread.

5. Sprinkle generously with salt and pepper.

6. Dot the surface with the butter and bake for 15 minutes or until the eggs are cooked to your liking.

7. Remove the dish from the oven and eat.

SOY SAUCE AND PEPPER FRIED EGGS

Prep 2 mins | Cook 5 mins | Serves 1

These could not be simpler, but are sublimely delicious, especially on soft buttered bread. My boys can't get enough of these admittedly messy but addictively delicious eggs. Prepare to meet your next food obsession. They're not just for breakfast either. Left to their own devices, my boys will happily cook lots of these eggs and eat them with rice for a simple but nourishing and satisfying lunch or dinner.

1 TBSP VEGETABLE OIL

1 LARGE KNOB BUTTER

2 EGGS (OR MORE)

A GENEROUS DASH DARK OR LIGHT SOY SAUCE
(I PREFER LIGHT BUT TRY BOTH AND
SEE FOR YOURSELF)

A GENEROUS PINCH GROUND BLACK PEPPER

1. Heat the oil together with the butter in a small pan.

2. When the butter melts and the mixture is moderately hot, break in the eggs and cook until the whites start to turn cloudy.

3. Add the soy sauce all over the eggs and follow with the pepper.

4. Allow the whites to set partially, then lightly stir the yolks and gently stir around to distribute the pepper and soy sauce but do not scramble the eggs.

5. Gently flip the eggs over and cook the other side for about 30 seconds.

6. Remove from the pan and drain off excess oil before serving immediately.

I know I'm supposed to encourage you to eat healthy, but you know what? That gunky butter/oil/soy sauce mix in the pan is insanely good mopped up with bread, especially buttered, cottony soft bread. Oh my! I won't tell your mum, if you don't…

CORNED BEEF AND EGG BREAKFAST HASH

Prep 10 mins | Cook 15 mins | Serves 4

This was my grandmother's weekend breakfast staple, with crusty bread and piping hot coffee. Leftovers, if any, were tossed into a wok, along with cold cooked rice and sliced spring onions, to make a very tasty, speedy and satisfying lunch. The reason I've given a recipe to feed four is that it makes little sense to cook half a can of corned beef and have the other half languishing and crusting over in the back of the fridge. Besides, with the suggestion for fried rice above and the possibility of luscious corned beef stuffed sandwiches in the offing, why would you want to cook half of anything?

4 TBSP VEGETABLE OIL

**1 LARGE ONION, PEELED, HALVED
    AND THICKLY SLICED**

2–4 RED CHILLIES, THICKLY SLICED

1 CAN CORNED BEEF

3–4 EGGS

PINCH OF SALT

PINCH OF GROUND BLACK PEPPER

LIME WEDGES (OPTIONAL)

1. Heat 3 tablespoons of the vegetable oil in a pan and sauté the onion until light brown but still crunchy.

2. Add the chillies and stir to heat through.

3. Break up the corned beef and add to the pan, stirring and mixing with the onion and chilli until the corned beef begins to get crusty.

4. Push the corned beef mixture to the side of the pan and the remaining oil to the pan.

5. Break the eggs into the pan and allow to partially set before scrambling lightly.

6. Combine the corned beef and eggs and stir until well mixed and eggs are done to your preference.

7. Season to taste with salt and pepper.

8. Divide the hash among four plates. Garnish each serving with a lime wedge, if you wish and serve hot with bread.

CHAI TOW KWAY

Prep 15 mins | Cook 15 mins | Serves 2 (well, actually 1... twice)

This delectable dish seems to truly stump western culinary sensibilities and the inevitable question, "But where's the carrot?!" Well, it's radish really, sweet, succulent radish or daikon. Finding the kind of radish rice cake used in traditional versions can be tricky, but when desperation strikes, you do the best you can. Your best bet would be Asian grocers, especially Vietnamese, Japanese or Korean ones or the Asian foods section in larger supermarkets. The legwork will be all worthwhile.

5 TBSP VEGETABLE OIL

300 G (1 PACKET) ASIAN RICE CAKE, CUT INTO SMALL CUBES

4 CLOVES GARLIC, BASHED, SKINS DISCARDED AND ROUGHLY CHOPPED

2 TBSP CHOPPED CHAI POH OR PICKLED RADISH (JAPANESE OR KOREAN)

1–2 TBSP PREPARED CHILLI PASTE (OPTIONAL)

1 TBSP LIGHT SOY SAUCE

PINCH OF SALT

PINCH OF PEPPER

2 EGGS, LIGHTLY BEATEN

1 STALK SPRING ONION WASHED, AND CUT INTO SHORT LENGTHS

1. Heat 2 tablespoons vegetable oil in a large shallow pan and when really hot, fry the rice cake cubes, stirring and turning them over so they brown evenly. Remove the rice cakes from the pan and set aside.

2. Heat another 3 tablespoons of oil in same pan and fry the garlic and pickled radish until light brown.

3. Add the chilli paste and cook until the oil seeps out, then add the rice cakes, soy sauce, salt and pepper and stir until well mixed.

4. Push the rice cakes to one side of the pan and pour in the eggs. Allow to set partially, then push the rice cakes over the eggs and stir and turn until the rice cakes are coated with eggs.

5. Add the spring onions and stir for a few more minutes until the eggs are completely cooked.

6. Dish out and serve immediately.

If you can't get Malaysia or Singapore style rice cake flavoured with grated radish, or yam (taro), use the Vietnamese or Korean versions. These rice cakes may be plain or flavoured with yam, carrot, radish or pumpkin. Any type you can find will work as long as it's fresh rice cake, not dehydrated versions.

If you cannot find chilli paste, use Korean gochujang. Other possibilities are Hainanese chicken rice chilli sauce or Indonesian sambal oelek. I prefer gochujang as some versions of Hainanese chilli sauces or Indonesian sambals available in the west can be dicey in terms of flavour.

ROTI JOHN
BEEF AND EGG TOPPED FRIED BREAD
Prep 15 mins | Cook 10 mins | Serves 2

Once upon a time, when Singapore was still a British colony, an English serviceman walked up to a hawker, and hankering for something closer to the food of his homeland, requested some bread and beef. Something probably got garbled in translation and what emerged was a split French loaf topped with a tasty mess of egg, minced beef and onion. We'll never know if it really was what the homesick Englishman actually wanted (or if this story is even true) but it was said that he seemed mightily pleased with it and wolfed it down happily. In honour of British servicemen in Singapore at the time, who were all referred to as "John" by locals, as apparently, one Englishman looked pretty much like another, the creation was christened "roti john" (John's bread). The rest, as they say, is oh, so delicious history.

1 LOAF BAGUETTE (30 CM LONG)
100 G MINCED BEEF
1 ONION, PEELED AND COARSELY CHOPPED
1 GREEN CHILLI, COARSELY CHOPPED
    (OPTIONAL)
½ TSP GROUND BLACK PEPPER
½ TSP SALT
2 LARGE EGGS
1–2 TBSP OIL

1. Vertically cut the loaf down the middle so you have two pieces, each measuring 15 cm, which can easily fit most pans. Horizontally split each half but do not cut through. The halves should open out like butterflies but still be attached together.

2. In a mixing bowl, combine the beef, onion, chilli, pepper, salt and eggs and stir until thoroughly combined.

3. Heat the oil in a well seasoned griddle or non-stick pan, until moderately hot.

4. Scoop up the egg and beef mixture and spread onto the cut surface of loaf halves, right up to the edges.

5. Quickly flip the bread over onto pan so that the beef and egg mixture is face down. Press down firmly with a spatula so that the topping sticks to bread, and cook until fragrant and edges are brown. This should take about 5 minutes over medium heat.

6. Slide the spatula carefully under the bread, scraping gently, until the bread loosens. Flip over and cook on the other side, again pressing down with the spatula so that the other side crisps up evenly.

7. Remove from the pan and close the two halves together so the egg and beef topping are now inside the bread.

8. Cool slightly, then cut each closed piece into 4 or 5 slices.

9. Serve immediately with sweet Thai chilli sauce or a mixture of half ketchup and half chilli sauce.

CHINESE PUMPKIN CAKE

Prep 20 mins | Cook 20 mins | Serves 4

I wish pumpkin puree were as easy to find in Singapore; making this would be so much easier! This is so much faster in the microwave, but you have to be watchful as mere minutes separate a successful pumpkin cake from a slab of yellow rubber. Do this when you're free on a Sunday, so you have a yummy breakfast waiting for you over the next few weekday mornings.

125 G (1¼ CUPS) RICE FLOUR

400 ML (2 CUPS) WATER

3 TBSP VEGETABLE OIL

4 CLOVES GARLIC, BASHED, SKINS DISCARDED
    AND ROUGHLY CHOPPED

A GENEROUS HANDFUL SMALL DRIED PRAWNS

½ TSP PEPPER

60 G (½ CUP) CANNED BUTTON MUSHROOMS,
    DRAINED AND SLICED

1 RED CHILLI, SLICED

250 G (1⅔ CUPS) CANNED UNSWEETENED
    PUMPKIN PUREE

1½ TSP SALT

1 STALK SPRING ONION WASHED AND SLICED

> Drizzle sesame oil, sweet thick dark soy sauce and chilli garlic oil (page 72) over the pumpkin cake, then sprinkle with toasted sesame seeds before eating, if you wish.
>
> Instead of microwaving, you could also steam this over boiling water, after pouring into the dish and covering the top with cling wrap. Steaming normally takes about 45 minutes.

1. Line a 23 cm ceramic pie dish with cling wrap, with generous overhang.

2. Combine the rice flour and water in a large bowl or measuring jug and stir until very smooth, then set aside.

3. Heat the vegetable oil in a large pan or wok. Add the garlic, prawns and pepper and fry until fragrant.

4. Add the mushrooms and chilli and stir for a few minutes.

5. Add the pumpkin puree and stir to combine with the other ingredients. Keep stirring until the puree thickens.

6. Stir the rice flour mixture and pour into the pan of pumpkin puree.

7. Add the salt and spring onions and stir until the mixture is thick and sticky.

8. Pour the mixture into the pie dish and level the top with a spatula. Cover the bowl loosely with more cling wrap, making sure the overhang is still outside the dish.

9. Cook in a microwave on "Medium" for 10–15 minutes or until it is firm to the touch.

10. Remove and leave to cool completely before lifting out using the plastic overhang. Slice and serve.

GERAGOK FRITTERS

KRILL FRITTERS

Prep 15 mins | Cook 10 mins | Makes 16–18

These are fantastic as afternoon snacks with tea or coffee though I grew up eating them piled over steaming hot rice and doused liberally with a hot and tangy chilli and vinegar sauce. Any true blue Singaporean Kristang (Portuguese descended Eurasian) will know what I'm talking about, but you will not find these easily outside of a Kristang home. Geragok is also an unflattering way of addressing a Portuguese Eurasian in the local context, which came about through association with the krill fishermen of Malacca, who were mostly Portuguese Eurasians. These days, though, the term is generally used and taken in good humour.

120 G (ABOUT 2 HANDFULS) FRESH KRILL

1 ONION, PEELED AND THINLY SLICED

1 TSP GROUND WHITE PEPPER

1 TSP SALT

½ TSP SUGAR

40 G (½ CUP) PLAIN OR ALL-PURPOSE FLOUR

40 G (½ CUP) RICE FLOUR

1 TSP BAKING POWDER

1 LARGE EGG

70 ML (⅓ CUP) WATER

300 ML (1½ CUPS OR ENOUGH TO ACHIEVE A DEPTH OF 4 CM IN THE PAN) VEGETABLE OIL

1. Pick over the krill and remove any impurities. Wash and drain thoroughly in a colander.

2. Put the drained krill in a large mixing bowl and add the onion, pepper, salt, sugar, flours and baking powder. Stir and toss until the krill is thoroughly coated. Stir in the egg and water and stop as soon as everything is thoroughly combined.

3. Heat the oil in a deep frying pan and when moderately hot, drop tablespoonfuls of the batter into the oil, allowing room for the fritters to puff up and cook without sticking to each other. Turn the fritters over to ensure even browning.

4. When golden and crisp, remove the fritters and drain on kitchen paper.

5. Serve immediately with your favourite tangy chilli sauce.

Krill are tiny shrimps, the kind that gets dried and made into belacan (fermented shrimp paste). They have an intensely savoury yet sweet flavour and are increasingly difficult to come by. If you can't get them, use a roughly equivalent amount of small peeled fresh prawns instead.

SIMPLIFIED YEW CHAR KWAY
FRIED DOUGH STICKS
Prep 15 mins | Rising 45 mins | Cook 10 mins Makes 12

How could something so simple inspire such devotion and be so ridiculously satisfying? I suppose only another Singaporean could understand. Just as the French cannot contemplate a day without their iconic croissant, each time I know I will be away from home for a while, I wish I could pack some yew char kway in with my toothbrush. Don't be intimidated by the thought of making these. There is a definite art to making them the traditional way, but this version really is very easy.

400 G (4 CUPS) PLAIN OR ALL-PURPOSE FLOUR
⅔ TSP INSTANT YEAST
1 TSP SUGAR
1½ TSP SALT
⅓ TSP BAKING SODA
250 ML (1¼ CUPS) WATER (SLIGHTLY WARM OR
    JUST A BIT OVER BODY TEMPERATURE)
400 ML (2 CUPS) OIL

1. Combine all ingredients except the oil (avoiding direct contact between the salt and the yeast) in a large mixing bowl. Knead until you have a smooth dough that doesn't stick to your hands.

2. Form the dough into a neat ball, oiling your hands lightly if necessary, to prevent sticking, and cover the bowl with a clean cloth or sheet of plastic. Leave to rise for 30–45 minutes or until it has doubled in volume.

3. Turn the dough out onto a clean, dry surface lightly dusted with flour. Pat down and roll out to a neat rectangle about 5 mm thick. Cover with cloth; and wait for about 5 minutes for dough to rest. Cut into 12 even strips about 15 cm by 3 cm.

4. Using the blunt side of a knife blade, press down the centre of each dough strip as if you're cutting it, but do not cut through the dough. There should be a deep impression but the dough strip should still be in one piece.

5. Heat the oil in a deep pan, until moderately hot. Gently lift the dough strip and lower into the hot oil. Repeat with the other dough strips, making the impression with the knife only immediately before frying each strip of dough so the impression remains and shows clearly after frying.

6. Turn the strips and push them into the oil so they cook right through and brown evenly. Don't fry too many at once as the temperature of the oil will drop, and this will cause the dough to absorb more oil and become greasy.

7. Remove from the pan when golden brown and drain on kitchen paper. Repeat with the remaining dough.

8. Serve immediately with black tea, Chinese tea, coffee or soy bean milk.

Yeast is organic and variable, so don't give up after one go if your first attempt is unsuccessful.

Ensure the water is lukewarm to be on the safe side as too high a temperature will kill the yeast. Better a little too cool than a little too warm.

Salt retards yeast and can even kill it so avoid directly combining the two together. It's best to mix your salt through the flour first, then add your yeast, or vice versa.

The rising time given is for warmer climates like the tropics, where yeast tends to take a shorter time to become active because of the ambient warmth and humidity. If you are making this in cooler climates, the rising time should be about an hour or possibly longer. Exact rising times are hard to predict, but the dough is sufficiently risen when it has at least doubled in volume, regardless of the time given in the recipe.

CURRY PUFFS

Prep 45 mins | Cook 25 mins | Makes about 10 puffs

Almost every culinary culture you could think of has its own version of this filled pastry parcel, whether it's an empanada, a turnover, or a pasty. Of course I prefer our version, with its spicy and fragrant filling encased in a crisp, blistered pastry shell. Few things satisfy more at tea time and the very first one you bite into, fresh and piping hot from the pan, will convince you that making them was time very well spent.

FILLING

4 TBSP LIGHT VEGETABLE OIL

1 LARGE ONION, PEELED AND FINELY DICED

**1½ TBSP MEDIUM HOT CURRY POWDER,
MIXED TO A PASTE WITH 3 TBSP WATER**

**1 LARGE YELLOW FLESHED POTATO, PEELED,
DICED AND SOAKED IN WATER TO
PREVENT DISCOLOURATION**

100 G MINCED CHICKEN, LAMB OR BEEF

1 TSP SALT

½ TSP SUGAR

100 ML (½ CUP) WATER

PASTRY

150 G (1½ CUPS) PLAIN OR ALL-PURPOSE FLOUR

⅓ TSP SALT

**50 G (⅓ CUP OR 4 GENEROUS TBSP) COLD
MARGARINE OR BUTTER, IN CUBES OR
SMALL PIECES**

50 ML (¼ CUP) COLD WATER

**300 ML (1½ CUPS OR ENOUGH TO ACHIEVE A
DEPTH OF 4 CM IN THE PAN) VEGETABLE OIL**

1. Prepare the filling first so it has time to cool. Heat the oil in a pan and when moderately hot, cook the onion until limp and fragrant.

2. Add the curry paste, potato and meat and stir, breaking up the meat and turning over everything to prevent burning.

3. When the meat changes colour, add the salt, sugar and water and stir, scraping the bottom of the pan to dislodge stuck-on bits.

4. Cover and cook over gentle heat until the potatoes are tender and the filling is thick and almost dry.

5. Turn off the heat and leave to cool while you make the pastry.

6. To make the pastry, whisk the flour and salt together in a large mixing bowl. Add the butter and rub into the flour with your finger tips, breaking up or squeezing into ever smaller pieces until the flour resembles coarse crumbs.

7. Pour in the water and lightly mix everything, pushing it all together to form a dough. **Avoid kneading the dough** to achieve a light and crisp texture.

8. Turn the dough out onto a lightly floured clean surface, roll out to a thickness of $2-3$ mm and cut out circles with a 7 cm round pastry or scone cutter. Divide the filling into as many portions as you have circles.

9. Put a portion on each circle, off-centre and lightly wet the edges of each pastry circle. Fold over each circle to enclose the filling and press down firmly on the edges to seal. Pinch and twist the edges at regular intervals to achieve a rope-like pattern.

10. Heat the oil for frying in a deep and small to medium pot. When moderately hot, fry the puffs a few at a time until golden, turning over a few times to ensure even cooking. Drain on crushed kitchen paper and serve while still hot.

If you have leftovers, store them wrapped in a brown paper bag, kitchen foil or baking paper in the refrigerator, for up to 2 days. Avoid storing in covered containers or sealed plastic as this will encourage condensation and result in a soggy crust. Before eating, unwrap and gently heat in a toaster oven for $8-10$ minutes or until hot and crusty again. If they darken too quickly, cover lightly with foil while reheating.

GARLIC BREAD

Prep 10 mins | Cook 25 mins | Serves 2 as a snack or 4 as a side

I am always suspicious of recipes that claim to be the best ever anything, but I will say that this is my best garlic bread recipe ever. There's no exotic or magical ingredient here, though the Parmesan does add a really nice punch of flavour—just don't go overboard on the garlic, make sure it's very finely minced (if you're using fresh) and be patient when you're toasting it. Nothing spoils a potentially great loaf of garlic bread more than impatience and insufficient toasting.

75 G (½ CUP) SOFT BUTTER
3 LARGE CLOVES GARLIC, PEELED AND
   FINELY MINCED
½ TSP DRIED OREGANO
45 G (½ CUP) FINELY GRATED PARMESAN CHEESE
1 SMALL BAGUETTE, SPLIT HORIZONTALLY
A GENEROUS PINCH OF SALT
A GENEROUS PINCH OF PEPPER

1. Preheat oven at 190°C.

2. Combine the butter, garlic, oregano and grated cheese in a mixing bowl. Stir until very thoroughly mixed.

3. Toast the baguette halves (cut side up) in the oven for about 8 minutes or until lightly crisp and golden. Remove from the oven and allow to cool slightly.

4. Divide the butter mixture into two portions and spread each portion evenly over the cut side of each toasted baguette half, to the very edge of the baguette.

5. Put the baguettes into the oven and toast again until the tops are golden and a wonderful aroma emits from the oven.

6. Remove from the oven, slice with a sharp serrated knife and serve immediately on its own, or with soup or pasta.

Try using 1 tablespoon prepared garlic paste or 2 teaspoons garlic powder, instead of freshly minced garlic cloves if you're in a hurry, too lazy to peel and mince your own garlic, or just don't like the smell of garlic on your hands. I promise, I won't judge you ;)

LOBAH

SHREDDED YAM AND MEAT ROLLS

Prep 20 mins | Cook 15 mins | Serves 3–4

If you like poh piah or yam puffs, you will probably love these simple to prepare yet very moreish rolls of shredded yam, pork and prawns. I like to make a huge pot of Japanese or Chinese tea before I sit down and tuck into these as the tannins in the tea are said to bind and flush fat out of your body (fingers crossed). Or you know what? Just eat two, if you can.

400 G YAM (TARO), PEELED AND FINELY
    SHREDDED (YOU SHOULD HAVE 300 G
    AFTER PEELING)
200 G MINCED PORK
200 G PRAWNS (SMALL ONES ARE FINE),
    SHELLED AND COARSELY CHOPPED
1 ONION, PEELED AND COARSELY CHOPPED
1 SMALL EGG
60 G (ABOUT ⅔ CUP) PLAIN OR
    ALL-PURPOSE FLOUR
1 TSP SALT
1 TSP SUGAR
½ TSP GROUND WHITE PEPPER
½ TSP CHINESE FIVE SPICE POWDER
    (OPTIONAL BUT A NICE AND VERY
    FRAGRANT ADDITION)
300 ML (1½ CUPS OR ENOUGH TO ACHIEVE A
    DEPTH OF 4 CM IN THE PAN) VEGETABLE OIL

1. In a large mixing bowl, combine all the ingredients together and knead until you have a workable paste, which has the consistency of a soft, slightly sticky dough.

2. Lightly flour your hands and form the paste into sausage-like logs or rolls about 10 cm long and 2.5 cm wide. Put the rolls onto a plate lightly dusted with flour to prevent them from sticking.

3. Heat up the oil in a deep pan and when moderately hot, gently lower in the rolls.

4. Fry until golden brown, turning occasionally, so they cook evenly. This normally takes about 6–8 minutes over medium heat. Remove from oil and drain on kitchen paper.

5. Cool slightly, then cut each roll diagonally into 2 or 3 pieces. Serve as it is or with your favourite chilli and garlic sauce or dip. And don't forget that big pot of tea!

If you cannot find yam, substitute with regular potatoes. White fleshed potatoes like Russet Burbank are best as they crisp up better than yellow fleshed potatoes when fried.

    Traditionally, thin matchstick-like strips of pork belly are used instead of minced pork, but it entails more work and requires a really sharp knife. If you're up to the challenge, use pork belly instead, but bear in mind you will have to fry the rolls longer as pork belly does not cook as quickly as minced pork.

    You can also form the paste into small flattened patties instead of large rolls. This way, they will cook much faster and you needn't worry about uncooked centres.

SOUPS

BAK KUT TEH

PORK RIB TEA

Prep 15 mins | Cook 2 hrs | Serves 2–3

You may be able to find ready-mixed bak kut teh spices in supermarkets or specialists Chinese or Asian grocers, but if you can't, this recipe will deliver the essence of what is good pork rib tea with minimum fuss and with commonly found herbs and spices.

2 LARGE STICKS CINNAMON

1 TBSP BLACK PEPPERCORNS, SPLIT WITH THE BACK OF A SPOON

3 WHOLE STAR ANISE

600 G MEATY PORK RIBS (EXCESS FAT TRIMMED OFF)

1 WHOLE HEAD UNPEELED GARLIC (USUALLY CONTAINS 10–12 INDIVIDUAL CLOVES)

1 CAN WHOLE BUTTON MUSHROOMS, DRAINED OR 1½ CUPS FRESH BUTTON MUSHROOMS, LIGHTLY RINSED

3 TBSP OYSTER SAUCE

2 TBSP LIGHT SOY SAUCE

2 TBSP DARK SOY SAUCE

1 TSP SUGAR

PINCH OF SALT

AS MUCH LETTUCE LEAVES AS YOU LIKE

PINCH OF PEPPER, TO GARNISH

DRIZZLE OF SESAME OIL, TO GARNISH

1. Combine cinnamon sticks, peppercorns and star anise in a piece of muslin or clean, thin handkerchief and tie securely into a knotted bag.

2. Put this bag into a large pot with all the other ingredients except the salt and lettuce, add enough water to cover meat and bring to a boil.

3. Reduce heat and simmer gently until ribs are tender. Skim off any scum that rises and discard to keep the soup clear.

4. Taste the soup and season to taste.

5. Turn off the heat and ladle into bowls of torn lettuce, garnish with a dash of pepper and a drizzle of sesame oil if you like.

6. Serve with white rice and a saucer of sliced red chilli in dark soy sauce.

This soup should be simmered for at least 1¼–1½ hours for the ribs to tenderise and for the flavours of the spices to come out and flavour both the broth and the meat. A little longer is better, but in most cases, unless the ribs are unusually tough, the meat will start to fall apart beyond 2 hours of simmering.

CHICKEN, CORN AND RED DATE SOUP

Prep 15 mins | Cook 1½ hrs | Serves 2–3

While I have been pretty fast and loose with my suggestions for canned, packaged, convenient and instant foods here and there in this book for the sake of convenience, please do not use canned or frozen corn here. Fresh corn adds a wonderful fragrance and sweetness which is the hallmark of this otherwise very simple soup. This is a favourite in my home. Try it and you'll see why.

3 WHOLE CHICKEN LEGS

3 EARS FRESH CORN, HUSKS AND SILK REMOVED
   AND EACH CUT ACROSS INTO 4 SECTIONS

5 SLICES GINGER, PEELED

1.2 L (6 CUPS) WATER

A GENEROUS HANDFUL DRIED RED DATES,
   RINSED AND DRAINED (OPTIONAL)

2 TSP SALT

PINCH OF PEPPER

1. Combine all ingredients in a large pot and bring to a boil.

2. Lower heat to minimum and simmer very gently for 1½ hours, skimming off and discarding any scum that rises.

3. Adjust seasoning if necessary.

4. Ladle soup into bowls and add a dash of white pepper before serving with rice and a saucer of sliced chillies in light or dark soy sauce.

You can also cook this in a slow cooker or crockpot. Combine all ingredients in slow cooker, reducing the amount of water to just enough to cover chicken legs. Cover and cook on "High" for 3 hours or on "Low" for 5 hours. Before serving, skim off any scum and adjust seasoning to taste.

CARROT, RADISH AND PORK RIB SOUP

Prep 10 mins | Cook 2 hrs | Serves 2

Not only do you get a delicious and healthy "tonic" broth to sip out of this, but after gentle, languid simmering, the ribs become all lusciously gooey tenderness. In Chinese herbalism, this is believed to be "cooling". The wolfberries or goji berries as they are known in the west, supposedly strengthen your eyes. But really, I cook this only because it's so darned delicious.

400 G MEATY PORK RIBS (EXCESS FAT
TRIMMED OFF)
1 MEDIUM CHINESE WHITE RADISH (DAIKON),
   PEELED AND THICKLY SLICED
2 MEDIUM CARROTS, PEELED AND THICKLY
   SLICED
2–3 TSP SALT
1 TSP SUGAR
50 G (½ CUP) WOLFBERRIES, RINSED AND
   DRAINED

1. Combine all ingredients except wolfberries in a deep pot.

2. Add enough water to cover the ribs. Bring to a boil, then lower heat and simmer for about 2 hours or until ribs are tender.

3. Skim off and discard the scum that rises to the top of the liquid to keep soup clear.

4. Add wolfberries for the last 15 minutes of simmering.

5. Taste and adjust seasoning if necessary.

6. Serve with rice and a saucer of sliced red chillies in dark soy sauce.

> You can also cook this in a slow cooker. Just combine all ingredients except wolfberries in slow cooker, cover and cook on "High" for 4 hours or "Low" for 6 hours. Add the wolfberries during the last 45 minutes of cooking. Before serving, skim off any scum and season to taste.

SLICED FISH AND LETTUCE SOUP

Prep 10 mins | Cook 15 mins | Serves 2

Any firm fleshed white fish will work in this soup. Tender flaky fish will crumble once the soup boils or even as you try to ladle the soup out of the pot. Look for varieties like snapper, garoupa (grouper), bream, orange roughy or mahi mahi. Fillets are best so you can just slice and drop them into your stock.

400 ML (2 CUPS) CANNED CHICKEN STOCK OR BROTH
1 SMALL PACK SOFT TOFU, CUBED
2 SMALL TOMATOES, QUARTERED
300 G FISH FILLETS, THICKLY SLICED ACROSS
1 VERY SMALL HEAD CRISP LETTUCE (ICEBERG VARIETY) CORE DISCARDED, LEAVES SEPARATED, WASHED AND TORN INTO LARGE PIECES
PINCH OF SALT
PINCH OF PEPPER
READY FRIED CRISP SHALLOTS, TO GARNISH

1. Put the stock to boil in a small pot.

2. Simmer for about a minute, then add fish slices and stir gently to prevent clumping.

3. As soon as the fish turns opaque (in about 30 seconds), add lettuce.

4. Season to taste with salt and pepper and turn off the heat as soon as lettuce wilts.

5. Ladle out into bowls and sprinkle with crisp shallots and extra pepper.

6. Serve immediately with rice and a saucer of sliced red chillies in light soy sauce.

SUP AYAM

Prep 15 mins | Cook 40 mins | Serves 2

This simple, homely and mildly spicy soup is really a simpler version of the more complicated Indonesian soto ayam, but it is still delicious. One sip and you will know why it's a favourite in local Malay households.

3 TBSP VEGETABLE OIL
1 LARGE ONION, PEELED, HALVED AND SLICED
3 CLOVES GARLIC, BASHED, SKINS DISCARDED
    AND ROUGHLY CHOPPED
5 CM GINGER, PEELED AND BASHED
2 WHOLE CHICKEN LEGS, EACH CUT INTO 2
    AT THE JOINT
1 LARGE POTATO, PEELED AND CUT INTO
    8 CHUNKS
1 SMALL CARROT, PEELED AND CUT INTO
    8 PIECES
500 ML (2½ CUPS) WATER
2 TSP SALT
½ TSP SUGAR
PINCH OF PEPPER
1 STALK CHINESE CELERY OR THE LEAFY TOPS
    OF REGULAR CELERY, TO GARNISH

1. Heat the vegetable oil in a pot and fry the onion, garlic and ginger until fragrant and the onions are limp.

2. Put in the chicken pieces, potato and carrot and stir for a few minutes.

3. Add water and bring to a boil.

4. Add salt and sugar then turn down the heat and simmer until the chicken and vegetables are tender.

5. Dish out and garnish with a dash of pepper and celery before serving. Serve hot with white rice and sambal belacan (page 44), sambal oelek or achar (page 67).

SUP KAMBING

SPICY INDIAN MUSLIM MUTTON SOUP

Prep 15 mins | Cook 4–8 hrs | Serves 3

A wonderfully warming and satisfying soup that really hits the spot on chilly evenings. This really is best eaten with cubes of baguette but feel free to ladle it over rice if you prefer, or try it with cooked noodles for a new and interesting twist. However you have it, be sure to give it a generous dash of pepper before slurping away. Go ahead, make as much noise as you want: an earthy, stick-to-your-ribs soup like this isn't meant to be sipped delicately!

3 TBSP VEGETABLE OIL

1 LARGE ONION, PEELED, HALVED AND THINLY SLICED

2 TBSP PREPARED GINGER PASTE

1 TBSP PREPARED GARLIC PASTE

500 G LAMB OR MUTTON CUBES (TRIM OFF EXCESS FAT IF YOU WISH)

1 TSP PEPPER POWDER

1 TBSP MILD CURRY POWDER OR KORMA CURRY POWDER

1 LARGE POTATO, PEELED AND CUT INTO SMALL CUBES

2 TSP SALT

READY FRIED CRISP SHALLOTS, TO GARNISH (OPTIONAL)

FRESH CORIANDER LEAVES, TO GARNISH (OPTIONAL)

1. Plug in your slow cooker, put in vegetable oil and, with the lid on, set it on "High".

2. When the oil is hot, put in the onion, ginger paste and garlic paste and stir around until fragrant and light brown.

3. Add in the meat cubes, pepper powder and curry powder and stir and turn the meat over until coated with spices.

4. Pour in enough hot water to just cover the meat and add potato and salt. Cover pot again and bring to a boil.

5. Lower the heat and leave undisturbed for 4 hours on "High" or 8 hours on "Low".

6. Test a few meat cubes with a fork (bite if you need to) to check for tenderness.

7. When tender, skim off any scum and adjust seasoning before turning off cooker and ladle out soup into bowls.

8. Garnish with crisp shallots, coriander leaves and a dash of pepper before serving.

Slow cooking turns the meat meltingly tender and removes the need to keep topping up the pot with water. But you can cook this over the stove if you don't have a slow cooker. Just reduce the cooking time to around 2½ hours and make sure the meat is always covered by liquid.

HOT AND SOUR SZECHUAN SOUP

Prep 15 mins | Cook 15 mins | Serves 2

Jaded appetites are instantly revived by this highly aromatic and robustly flavoured spicy soup. If your appetite has been blunted by illness, fatigue or just boredom with eating the same kinds of food, give this easy and palate-awakening soup a try.

600 ML (3 CUPS) CANNED CHICKEN STOCK OR
   BROTH
2 BAMBOO SHOOT HALVES (PACKED IN WATER),
   DRAINED AND THINLY SLICED
1 CHICKEN BREAST, SKINNED, HALVED AND
   CUT INTO THIN STRIPS
4 FRESH SHIITAKE MUSHROOMS, STEMMED
   AND THINLY SLICED
2 TBSP BLACK VINEGAR
1 TBSP CHILLI GARLIC OIL (PAGE 72)
2 TBSP CORNSTARCH
1 SMALL PACK SOFT TOFU, CUBED
PINCH OF SALT
PINCH OF PEPPER
SESAME OIL, TO GARNISH
FRESH CORIANDER LEAVES, TO GARNISH

1. Put the stock into a pot and bring to a boil.

2. Add the bamboo shoots, chicken, mushrooms, vinegar and chilli garlic oil and stir so chicken strips don't clump together.

3. Bring to a boil, then dissolve cornstarch in about 3 tablespoons cold water and gently stir into soup.

4. Simmer until thickened, then add tofu and gently stir through and cook for another 2 minutes or so.

5. Add salt and pepper to taste before turning off heat.

6. Ladle into bowls and garnish with sesame oil and coriander leaves before serving.

For a slight variation, lightly beat 1 egg and stir into soup after adding cornstarch and water mixture and before adding tofu.

EASY TOMATO RASAM

Prep 10 mins | Cook 15 mins | Serves 2

In many local south Indian homes, rasam is taken almost daily as it's believed to awaken the appetite, aid digestion as well as prevent and treat illness. This version is not terribly authentic, but tastes close to how an Indian mother would make it, and uses ingredients you can find almost anywhere. So if your palate is jaded with the same old fare, give it a kick up with this punchy yet super easy soup.

3 LARGE CLOVES GARLIC, PEELED

2 TBSP VEGETABLE OIL

1 ONION, PEELED AND THINLY SLICED

**600 ML (3 CUPS) READY MADE CHICKEN OR
    VEGETABLE STOCK**

**3 MEDIUM SIZED RIPE TOMATOES, CUT INTO
    WEDGES OR JUST SQUASHED AND HAND
    BROKEN INTO QUARTERS**

**1 TSP CUMIN SEEDS, LIGHTLY TOASTED THEN
    CRUSHED WITH THE BACK OF A SPOON**

1 TSP CHILLI POWDER

1 TSP GROUND BLACK PEPPER

½ TSP TURMERIC POWDER

**2 TBSP FRESHLY SQUEEZED LIME JUICE
    (OR TO TASTE)**

**⅔ TSP SALT (OR TO TASTE – BE CAREFUL AS
    READY MADE STOCK CAN BE QUITE SALTY)**

CORIANDER LEAVES TO GARNISH (OPTIONAL)

1. Toast the whole garlic cloves in a toaster oven until evenly browned all over and beginning to char in places. It shouldn't be burnt, however, or your soup will be bitter. Set aside.

2. Heat 2 tablespoons of oil in a pot and fry the onion until golden and fragrant. Pour in the chicken stock and bring to a boil.

3. Squash the toasted garlic and add to the pot with the tomatoes, cumin seeds, chilli powder, black pepper, turmeric powder and lime juice.

4. Bring back to a boil. Lower the heat and simmer for 2 minutes or just until the tomatoes soften.

5. Taste and add salt if needed. Turn off the heat and ladle into bowls. Garnish with coriander and serve with rice, other Indian dishes and crisp, deep fried pappadums (Indian rice and lentil crackers) if you can find them.

Dark toasted garlic is a very good substitute for perungayam, hing or asafoetida (a pungent plant resin used in Indian cooking), which is essential for that characteristic rasam flavour, but practically impossible to find in the West.

SEAFOOD

ASSAM FISH CURRY

PRAWN OMELETTE

STEAMED FISH WITH GINGER, SPRING ONION
AND SOY SAUCE

EASY FISH OTAH

BLACK PEPPER AND ONION TUNA

PRAWN SAMBAL

SARDINE AND TOMATO CURRY

STIR FRIED PRAWNS IN GARLIC AND BLACK
BEAN SAUCE

ASSAM FISH CURRY

Prep 10 mins | Cook 20 mins | Serves 2

You probably think assam fish curry is too much of a bother to cook in a small, basics-only kitchen like yours, and you would be right, if you're thinking of your mum's or grandmother's family secret version. Of course I'm not going to say this is like mum's, but it does have everything you love about the spicy, tangy and robust goodness of Singapore's favourite fish curry, and it's a whole lot easier and faster to put together. Quick, try now!

5 TBSP VEGETABLE OIL

**1 SMALL ONION, PEELED, HALVED AND
    FINELY CHOPPED**

2 TBSP PREPARED GINGER PASTE

1 TBSP PREPARED GARLIC PASTE

2–3 TBSP PREPARED CHILLI PASTE

1 TBSP FISH SAUCE

1 TSP SALT

200 ML (1 CUP) WATER

**400 G (ABOUT 4 PIECES) WHITE FISH FILLETS
    (BREAM, TILAPIA, SOLE, COD OR JOHN DORY)**

50 ML (¼ CUP) UNSWEETENED LIME JUICE

2 SMALL TOMATOES, QUARTERED

**1 HANDFUL VIETNAMESE MINT LEAVES (KESUM,
    POLYGONUM OR LAKSA LEAVES), TO GARNISH**

1. Heat the vegetable oil in a pot and, when hot, fry the onion, ginger, garlic and chilli paste until fragrant and the oil seeps out.

2. Add fish sauce, salt and water and bring to a boil

3. Lower the heat, gently lower in the fish and simmer until the fish turns opaque.

4. Add lime juice and tomato quarters and stir gently. Taste and adjust seasoning if necessary.

5. After 1–2 minutes, add the mint leaves and turn off the heat.

6. Dish out over the white rice and serve.

Achar (page 67) complements this dish very well.

A stalk or two of fresh lemongrass will make a world of difference, if you can find it. If using, cut off the top ⅔, remove coarse outer leaves and bash the bottoms until they crack open. Fry these in the pot before adding anything else then proceed with the recipe. If you can only find dried lemongrass, don't bother. It's a poor substitute. If you can't get Vietnamese mint, try using fresh basil (Italian or Thai) leaves or mint leaves instead. Whatever you use, make sure it's fresh. Dried ones are honestly a waste of time in this case.

PRAWN OMELETTE

Prep 10 mins | Cook 10 mins | Serves 2

Sometimes, the simplest things are the most delicious. Sweet, succulent prawns, tender perfectly cooked eggs, the spicy aroma of pepper and fragrant nuttiness of sesame oil. This is lovely with rice, and absolutely perfect with plain congee.

3 TBSP VEGETABLE OIL

200 G PRAWNS, SHELLED

1 STALK SPRING ONION WASHED, DRAINED AND SLICED

1 TSP SALT

⅓ TSP SUGAR

4 EGGS, LIGHTLY BEATEN

1 TSP SESAME OIL

¼ TSP PEPPER

2 TBSP WATER

1. Heat the vegetable oil in a frying pan or wok.

2. When hot, add the prawns and stir over high heat until they turn red/pink.

3. Add the spring onion and stir for a few seconds.

4. Combine the remaining ingredients and whisk to dissolve salt and sugar.

5. Pour the egg mixture over the prawns in the pan and swirl around to evenly coat the pan or wok.

6. Allow the eggs to cook over medium heat until half set, then cut with the edge of a kitchen spatula, into quarters.

7. Flip over each quarter and cook the other side for about 1 minute.

8. Transfer to a plate and serve immediately.

STEAMED FISH WITH GINGER, SPRING ONION AND SOY SAUCE

Prep 10 mins | Cook 10 mins | Serves 2

Sometimes you've got to indulge yourself and give your body what it wants, and sometimes, you have to ignore your cravings and give your body what it needs. Even though this is healthy and figure friendly, it doesn't mean that you won't enjoy eating it. Just be sure you don't overcook the fish and you'll definitely relish every sweet and succulent morsel.

400 G FRESH WHITE FISH FILLETS (BREAM, SOLE, SNAPPER OR DORY)

½ TBSP SESAME OIL

4 SLICES GINGER, PEELED AND FINELY SHREDDED

2½ TBSP LIGHT SOY SAUCE

PINCH OF PEPPER, TO GARNISH

1 STALK SPRING ONION, CUT INTO FINE SHREDS OR INTO SHORT LENGTHS, TO GARNISH

1. Fill a large pot or wok ⅔ full with water and put in a wide and shallow upturned bowl.

2. Cover and let the water boil.

3. Put the well drained fish fillet on a slightly curved plate (so the juices don't spill out) that will fit into the wok or pot.

4. Cut a few slashes into each fillet with a sharp knife and drizzle fish with sesame oil.

5. Scatter the ginger over the fillets.

6. When water boils, put the fish into pot or wok on the upturned bowl, then cover and steam for 8 minutes.

7. Open the cover and if the fish is opaque and flakes easily when pierced with a fork, drizzle evenly with the soy sauce.

8. Turn off the heat and remove plate from wok.

9. Garnish with the pepper and spring onions and serve immediately with white rice and a saucer of sliced red chillies in light soy sauce and lime juice.

EASY FISH OTAH

Prep 15 mins | Cook 20–30 mins | Serves 4

Aren't you glad you learned to cook nasi lemak (page 93)? Here's another gorgeous dish to pair it with. You could steam or bake this. If you like it soft and moist, steam it. If you prefer a bit of browning and a light crust, bake it. You're the boss!

4 EGGS
200 ML (1 CUP) THICK COCONUT MILK
2–3 TBSP TOM YUM PASTE
1 TSP SALT
1 TSP SUGAR
1 TSP TUMERIC POWDER
1 TBSP RICE FLOUR
A GENEROUS HANDFUL FRESH BASIL LEAVES
    (ITALIAN OR THAI), FINELY SHREDDED
500 G FISH FILLET, THINLY SLICED (WHITE FISH
    LIKE BREAM, SNAPPER OR DORY)

> To bake, preheat oven at 180°C before you start preparing the dish. Generously brush the inside of a medium-sized baking dish with oil. Pour the prepared mixture into dish and bake for 30 minutes or until firm in the middle. Remove from oven and cool before cutting.

1. Fill a big pot or wok ⅔ full with water and put an upturned, wide and shallow bowl in it.

2. Cover and bring the water to a boil.

3. Combine everything except fish in a large mixing bowl and stir until it is well mixed and lump free.

4. Add the fish slices and gently stir through.

5. Pour the mixture into a small and shallow rectangular or round casserole dish that will fit inside your pot or wok.

6. Cover the casserole with cling wrap and steam for about 25 minutes or until set.

7. Turn off the heat and remove the dish carefully.

8. Cool before cutting or scooping out with a spoon.

BLACK PEPPER AND ONION TUNA

Prep 5 mins | Cook 10 mins | Serves 2

Try to get oil packed tuna as it is tastier and more succulent than water packed tuna. The few extra calories are well worth it! This goes equally well with plain white rice, boiled and drained macaroni, creamy mashed potato or as a very tasty and spicy sandwich filling.

3 TBSP VEGETABLE OIL

**1 MEDIUM ONION, PEELED, HALVED
    AND SLICED**

2 CANS (185 G EACH) TUNA (DRAIN OFF OIL)

1 TBSP BLACK PEPPERCORNS, COARSELY GROUND

PINCH OF SALT

SQUEEZE OF LIME OR LEMON JUICE

1. Heat the vegetable oil in a pan or wok until it is hot but not smoking.

2. Cook the onion until golden and fragrant.

3. Reduce the heat to medium and add in the tuna and pepper, stirring until the tuna is well-mixed.

4. Squeeze over the lime or lemon juice and add salt if desired.

5. Stir and turn off the heat. Serve with rice, bread, mashed potato or pasta.

PRAWN SAMBAL

Prep 10 mins | Cook 15 mins | Serves 2–3

This is a cracker of a combination with nasi lemak (page 93), or if you chop up the prawns coarsely before cooking, makes a fantastic, spicy filling for sandwiches. Ready peeled raw prawns are easily available in the frozen foods section of supermarkets and I definitely recommend that you look for them as peeling prawns is really quite fiddly. If you're lucky, you may even find fresh peeled prawns, waiting to be turned into this delightfully spicy treat.

250 G PRAWNS, SHELLED

4 TBSP VEGETABLE OIL

1 SMALL TO MEDIUM ONION, PEELED, HALVED
    AND FINELY CHOPPED

2 TSP PREPARED GARLIC PASTE

3–4 TBSP PREPARED CHILLI PASTE

2 TSP FISH SAUCE

1 TSP SUGAR

½ TSP SALT

SQUEEZE OF LIME JUICE (THIS DISH SHOULD
    NOT BE PERCEPTIBLY SOUR)

1. If the prawns have a dark vein down their back, slit the backs open and remove, then rinse and drain thoroughly. I recommend smaller prawns as they usually have no dark veins.

2. Heat vegetable oil and add the well drained prawns and stir till they turn pink/red. Remove the prawns and set aside.

3. Add onion, garlic and chilli paste to the same pan and stir over medium heat until fragrant and the oil seeps out.

4. Return the prawns and juices back to pan and add fish sauce, sugar and salt.

5. Stir well to mix and taste. Adjust the taste if necessary, turn off the heat and stir in the lime juice.

6. Dish out and serve.

SARDINE AND TOMATO CURRY

Prep 10 mins | Cook 15 mins | Serves 2

I used to eat this very often as a teenager, left to my own devices in my mum's big scary kitchen, full of sharp knives and huge pans. Growing up with only a grandmother and a working mother, I was forced to be independent when my grandmother died a few months before I turned 13. Mum had to do countless shifts and couldn't always prepare my meals before leaving for work. On those days when there was no lunch waiting for me on the table, I would open a can of sardines and get out the curry powder to make this simple but scrumptious curry that my mum taught me.

5 TBSP VEGETABLE OIL

1 MEDIUM ONION, PEELED, HALVED
　　AND SLICED

2 GREEN CHILLIES, THINLY SLICED (OPTIONAL)

2 ROUNDED TBSP MEDIUM HOT CURRY POWDER

2 TBSP PLAIN UNSWEETENED YOGHURT

100 ML (½ CUP) WATER

1 LARGE CAN SARDINES IN TOMATO SAUCE
　　(DISCARD SAUCE AS IT'S FISHY)

2 TOMATOES, QUARTERED

1 TSP SALT

1. Heat the vegetable oil in a pot, wok or deep pan until hot but not smoking.

2. Put in the onion and green chillies and stir around until the onions are golden and the mixture is fragrant.

3. Add in the curry powder, yoghurt and water all at once and stir quickly until the mixture boils and thickens slightly.

4. Add in the sardines and tomatoes, stir gently and bring back to a simmer.

5. Season to taste, stir, then turn off heat and dish out. Serve with rice, baguette or flat bread

STIR FRIED PRAWNS IN GARLIC AND BLACK BEAN SAUCE

Prep 20 mins | Cook 10 mins | Serves 2–3

If you get a hankering for this, you'll likely have to pay a tidy sum to get a decent plateful at a midrange restaurant. Chances are, you won't find anything resembling our beloved tze char stalls, except back here, on home turf. Don't sweat it! It's really easy to prepare. I'll show you how and you'll no longer be held hostage by overcharging, under-delivering 'Chinese' restaurants.

400 G PRAWNS, SHELLED AND THOROUGHLY DRAINED
1 ½ TBSP CORNFLOUR
½ TSP WHITE PEPPER
1 TBSP SESAME OIL
4 CLOVES GARLIC, PEELED AND CHOPPED
1 WHITE ONION, PEELED AND THICKLY SLICED
1 SMALL RED CAPSICUM (RED BELL PEPPER), CORED AND CUT INTO SMALL SQUARES
1 ½ TBSP PREPARED GARLIC BLACK BEAN SAUCE (FROM A JAR)
⅓ TSP SUGAR
50 ML (¼ CUP) WATER
CORIANDER LEAVES TO GARNISH

1. Sprinkle the prawns with the cornflour and pepper and toss until they are evenly coated with flour.

2. Heat enough oil in a pan or wok until very hot. Fry the prawns in 2 batches over high heat, turning over often until they turn pink and are crusty. Remove from the pan and drain on kitchen paper.

3. Remove most of the oil from the pan, leaving behind about 2 tablespoons. Add the sesame oil and fry the garlic over moderate heat until fragrant.

4. Add the onion and capsicum and stir over high heat until the onion is fragrant and beginning to wilt. Stir in the black bean sauce and sugar until the capsicum is coated with black bean sauce.

5. Return the prawns to the pan and stir well. Add water if thick, then stir and turn off the heat. Dish out the mixture and garnish with coriander leaves.

6. Serve immediately with rice.

MEAT AND CHICKEN

EASY CHINESE FIVE SPICE ROAST CHICKEN

Prep 15 mins | Cook 50 mins | Serves 4 hungry or 6 polite diners

What a gladdening and reassuring sight is a perfectly roasted whole chicken, sitting on its platter, wafting inviting aromas around the table and awakening the most jaded of appetites! It was Henry IV of France who famously declared that as long as he was King, every working man in his kingdom would have a chicken in his pot every Sunday. Today, while being easily within the reach of all and sundry, a whole roast chicken is still something of a treat. This beautifully fragrant and tasty dish is a staple of Chinese restaurants in Singapore but is blessedly simple to do at home.

1 WHOLE CHICKEN (1.2–1.4 KG)
2–2½ TSP CHINESE FIVE SPICE POWDER
**2 TSP GARLIC SALT OR 1½ TSP REGULAR SALT
    (GARLIC SALT MAKES IT MUCH TASTIER)**
1 TSP PEPPER
1 TSP SUGAR

1. The chicken should have its feet, head and neck removed, but if not, cut these off. Remove all internal organs and wash inside and out until the water runs clear.

2. Drain the chicken in a colander for about 15 minutes to allow as much water as possible to run off.

3. While the chicken is draining, preheat oven at 230°C.

4. Combine all the remaining ingredients in a small, dry bowl and rub them together with your fingertips so that the flavours really mingle.

5. Sprinkle seasoning into the cavity, all over the front and back and under the skin of the breast. Rub well into the flesh and the skin of the chicken.

6. If you can manage it, loosen the skin from around the legs and thighs and sprinkle seasoning under the skin. Rub well into the flesh. Try not to tear the skin, especially on the breast.

7. Tuck the wing tips behind the chicken and place it breast side down (the best way to keep the breast really moist) in a roasting tray or tin and roast in a hot oven for 20 minutes.

8. Reduce heat to 180°C and continue to roast for 15 minutes (20 minutes if the chicken is larger).

9. Turn the chicken over so it is now breast side up and roast a further 15 minutes. Remove from the oven and allow the chicken to rest for 15–20 minutes before carving.

Roasting the chicken breast side down for most of the cooking time may result in a flattened breast, but it yields incredibly juicy and tasty breast meat, so I highly recommend it.

The generous layer of seasoning and high initial cooking temperature should ensure that the chicken does not stick to the pan, but sometimes, the skin might tear off when you try to turn the chicken over. It will still be delicious but if looks matter to you, put a roasting rack into the baking tray and put the chicken breast down on the rack. This will solve the problem.

The juices that collect in the baking tray are incredibly tasty and wonderful drizzled over the chicken, once cut.

GU LU YOKE

CANTONESE SWEET AND SOUR PORK

Prep 25 mins | Cook 20 mins | Serves 2–3

I must admit that I am not a fan of most restaurant versions of this though I blame not the dish itself, but poor execution and the usually recycled cooking oil many restaurants use for deep-frying the pork to save on food costs. Pork fillet or tenderloin is not usually used, but I prefer it for quick cooking and guaranteed tenderness; this is after all, sweet and sour pork, not sweet and sour chewing gum. The Worcestershire and oyster sauces are further personal touches to round out the flavour and add a little complexity to the base flavour notes of sweet and sour.

You can replace pork with boneless chicken cubes, beef tenderloin cubes or large shelled prawns.

300 G PORK TENDERLOIN OR FILLET, CUT INTO
  CUBES OF ABOUT 2 CM
1 TSP SALT
2 TSP SUGAR
½ TSP PEPPER
1 EGG
25 G (¼ CUP) CORN FLOUR, PLUS EXTRA FOR
  DUSTING PORK
300 ML (1½ CUPS OR ENOUGH TO ACHIEVE A
  DEPTH OF 4 CM IN THE PAN) VEGETABLE OIL
1 ONION, PEELED, CUT INTO LARGE CUBES AND
  LAYERS SEPARATED
1 SMALL GREEN BELL PEPPER (CAPSICUM),
  STALK, WHITE PITH AND SEEDS DISCARDED,
  THEN CUT INTO 2 CM CHUNKS
2 TSP WHITE VINEGAR
2 TBSP TOMATO KETCHUP
1 TBSP SWEET CHILLI SAUCE
3–4 DASHES WORCESTERSHIRE SAUCE
  (PREFERABLY LEA AND PERRINS)
2 TBSP OYSTER SAUCE
70 ML (⅓ CUP) WATER
1 SMALL JAPANESE CUCUMBER, PEELED,
  QUARTERED LENGTHWISE, CORE DISCARDED
  AND CUT INTO 2 CM CHUNKS
1 LARGE FIRM TOMATO, SLICED INTO 8 PIECES
  AND SEEDS DISCARDED
1 STALK SPRING ONION, CUT INTO 2 CM
  LENGTHS, TO GARNISH

1. Combine the pork, **half of the salt and sugar**, pepper, egg and corn flour in a large bowl and mix everything thoroughly by hand. Refrigerate for 30 minutes or leave on counter for 20 minutes.

2. Heat the oil for frying until moderately hot. Toss the marinated pork cubes in the extra corn flour until well coated. Shake off excess corn flour and fry the pork until crisp. Remove from the pan and drain on crushed kitchen paper. If you have a small pan, do this in two batches.

3. Remove almost all the oil from the pan and reheat pan, which should be coated with a layer of oil. Fry the onion and bell pepper until they change colour.

4. Combine the remaining salt and sugar, vinegar, ketchup, chilli sauce, Worcestershire sauce, oyster sauce and water and pour into pan. Stir and bring to a boil quickly.

5. Add the cucumber and tomato, stir and bring back to a simmer. Add the pork, stir and adjust seasoning if necessary.

6. Dish out, garnish with the spring onion and serve immediately with steamed white rice.

EURASIAN CHICKEN STEW

Prep 20 mins | Cook 40 mins | Serves 4

When it's raining, when I'm down or when I want something virtuously simple, yet soul satisfyingly good, this is where my very Singaporean, very Kristang soul goes. If ever a pot held comfort, this stew would be in it.

3 TBSP OIL

1 STICK CINNAMON

6 LARGE WHOLE CLOVES

1 LARGE ONION, PEELED AND THINLY SLICED

4 WHOLE CHICKEN LEGS (THIGHS AND DRUMSTICKS ATTACHED TOGETHER) EACH CUT INTO 2 AT THE JOINT

4 SMALL POTATOES, PEELED AND QUARTERED

2 MEDIUM CARROTS, PEELED AND CUT INTO CHUNKS

3 CUPS WATER OR CHICKEN STOCK

¼ SMALL CABBAGE, LEAVES SEPARATED AND RIBS DISCARDED

2 TSP SALT (USE LESS IF YOU'RE USING STOCK INSTEAD OF WATER)

PINCH OF PEPPER

1 STALK SPRING ONION, CUT INTO 4 CM LENGTHS, TO GARNISH

1. Heat the oil in a deep pan or pot and when moderately hot, add the cinnamon and cloves. Stir for about a minute to release their aromas. Add the sliced onions and cook over moderate heat, stirring often, until the onions are soft and translucent.

2. Add the chicken, potatoes and carrots and cook for about 5 minutes, until chicken pieces are evenly browned. Stir occasionally to prevent burning.

3. Pour in the water or stock, bring to a boil and reduce heat. Cover the pan or pot and simmer gently for about 20 minutes or until the chicken is no longer pink at the bone. Turn the chicken pieces over a few times for even cooking.

4. Add the cabbage leaves, pushing down into the liquid, and continue cooking until cabbage is tender about 3–5 minutes.

5. Season the stew to taste with salt and pepper. Dish out and garnish with spring onions before serving with white rice and sambal belacan (see recipe below).

Sambal belacan, a sharp, hot relish of red chillies, toasted belacan (fermented shrimp paste) and lime juice, really completes Eurasian chicken stew. If you can find a pestle and mortar, pound 3 red chillies, 2 teaspoons toasted crumbled belacan or Korean anchovy soup powder and 1 clove garlic to a paste and add 1 pinch each of sugar and salt to taste. Transfer to a relish saucer and add a squeeze of lime juice.

If you can't find a pestle and mortar, combine 1 tablespoon gochujang, 1 teaspoon anchovy powder and as much lime juice as you like. Stir well, then taste and add a little water if too salty.

NO ROAST CHAR SIEW

Prep 10 mins | Cook 50 mins | Serves 3

You may be thinking of specialist Cantonese meat roasters and expensive ovens right now, but you can actually make luscious, sticky and tender char siew in your kitchen very easily. It won't be like the char siew you see atop your favourite wonton noodles back home, all crusted and charred outside, but it will taste very nearly as good. The most important thing is to make sure you get the right cut of meat called "wu hua rou" in Mandarin, which can be meat from the shoulder, collar or belly of the pig. I like to use collar as it's less fatty than the other bits but still tasty and tender.

500 G PORK COLLAR (THE CUT FROM JUST BEHIND THE NECK OF THE PIG)
1 TBSP LIGHT SOY SAUCE
1 TBSP DARK SOY SAUCE
75 G (½ CUP) SUGAR
1 TSP SALT
350 ML (1¾ CUPS) WATER
¼ TSP RED FOOD COLOURING OR ANNATTO POWDER (OPTIONAL)
3 TBSP VEGETABLE OIL

1. Combine the pork, light and dark soy sauces, sugar, salt, water and colouring in a large mixing bowl and mix well.

2. Cover and refrigerate for 2 hours so that the surface of pork absorbs the red colour.

3. Remove from fridge and pour the marinade liquid into a pot.

4. Bring to a boil, then add in the meat and return to a boil.

5. Lower the heat to a simmer and cook until the liquid thickens and coats the meat all over.

6. Turn the meat over from time to time while simmering for even cooking and colour absorption.

7. Pour in the oil and turn the meat for a few minutes to coat so it looks shiny.

8. When the meat is almost dry and glossy looking, turn off the heat.

9. Transfer to a plate, cool, then slice.

Annatto is a seed and is available in powder form that is used as a natural food colour. It has almost no flavour but imparts an attractive deep reddish orange to foods. You can opt to leave out the colouring in this recipe altogether. It won't look as pretty, but it will still taste fabulous.

"Wu hua rou" means "five flower pattern" or "five petal pattern", referring to the fat distribution in these specific cuts of meat. When the cut of meat is sliced across the grain, the slices look like a flower with five petals outlined by a layer of fat.

FRAGRANT PORK BALLS WITH NAPA CABBAGE

Prep 15 mins | Cook 6 mins | Serves 2–3

Succulent meatballs and cabbage make a complete meal that would impress even your mother, but couldn't be easier! Imagine making mud pies then nuking them in the microwave. What fun! But, even better, these are definitely way more delicious.

300 G MINCED PORK (SUBSTITUTE WITH
   CHICKEN IF YOU PREFER)
200 G PRAWNS, SHELLED AND
   ROUGHLY CHOPPED
1½ TSP SALT
1½ TSP SUGAR
1 TBSP SESAME OIL
½ TSP PEPPER
1½ TBSP CORN FLOUR
¼ SMALL NAPA CABBAGE, CUT INTO CHUNKS
   AND ROOT STUMP DISCARDED
2 TBSP LIGHT SOY SAUCE
1 TSP SESAME OIL

> No microwave? Don't like the microwave? Steam over furiously boiling water for 12 minutes. Make sure meatballs are no longer pink inside before serving.

1. Combine the pork, prawns, salt, sugar, sesame oil, pepper and corn flour in a bowl.

2. Stir until thoroughly combined and form into 12 equal-sized meatballs.

3. Lay the cabbage in an even layer inside a wide and shallow bowl that will fit your microwave.

4. Arrange the meatballs in one layer over cabbage, then drizzle with soy sauce and 1 teaspoon sesame oil.

5. Cover the bowl with cling wrap and cut a small opening in the wrap to act as a steam vent so that it won't rupture while cooking.

6. Cook in a microwave on "Medium" for 3 minutes. Open the wrap and shift the meatballs around.

7. Reseal with the wrap and cook another 3 minutes on "Medium". Cut one meatball in half to ensure that the centre is no longer pink. If still pink, reseal with wrap and cook another 2 minutes on "Medium" or until done.

8. Remove the wrap and serve with white rice, plain boiled and drained instant noodles or rice congee.

EASY SOUTHEAST ASIAN CHICKEN CURRY

Prep 10 mins | Cook 20 mins | Serves 2–4

This is the curry to eat with nasi lemak (page 93). Any leftover gravy is wonderful for curry mee, along with bean sprouts, sliced fried fish cakes, sliced fried bean curd, a dollop of fried chilli paste and mint or basil leaves. I can't think of a better curry to have in your kitchen arsenal for sheer versatility.

4 CHICKEN BREAST HALVES, CUT INTO 2 CM
    CUBES
1 SMALL BRINJAL (OR EGGPLANT), TOPS
    DISCARDED AND CUT INTO CUBES SLIGHTLY
    LARGER THAN CHICKEN
3 TBSP TOM YUM PASTE
1 TSP TUMERIC POWDER
100 ML (½ CUP) THICK COCONUT MILK
1 TSP SALT
½ TSP SUGAR
FRESH BASIL LEAVES OR VIETNAMESE MINT
    LEAVES, TO GARNISH

1. Combine all ingredients, except for the basil or mint leaves, in a pot and pour in just enough water to only cover the meat.

2. Stir to dissolve the tom yum paste.

3. Bring slowly to a boil, then reduce heat and simmer until the chicken and brinjal are tender. They should cook in about the same time.

4. Taste and adjust the seasoning if necessary.

5. Turn off the heat and serve garnished with the herbs.

Make sure the brinjal has tight, fresh and plump looking skin with no blemishes or holes, no matter how tiny. These tiny holes are the bore marks of pests that burrow into the brinjal and lay their eggs inside. These eggs hatch into grubs, which is what you will see inside if you cut into a brinjal with holes on its skin. Slimmer brinjals are less likely to have chewy, slightly bitter seeds.

QUICK COTTAGE PIE

Prep 30 mins | Cook 40 mins | Serves 4

There's often confusion between shepherd's pie and cottage pie. Shepherds take care of sheep so shepherd's pie has lamb in it. Cottage pie is not for shepherds, hence there is no lamb in it. What's a substitute for lamb then? Why beef of course! But, what if shepherds love their little sheep babies so much that they refuse to eat lamb and insist their pies have only beef inside?!? Oh, never mind.

FILLING

3 TBSP VEGETABLE OIL
1 ONION, PEELED, HALVED AND
   ROUGHLY CHOPPED
500 G MINCED BEEF
2 TBSP PLAIN FLOUR
2 TBSP TOMATO PASTE
1 TBSP WORCESTERSHIRE SAUCE OR
   LIGHT SOY SAUCE
⅔ TSP MIXED DRIED HERBS
300 ML (1½ CUPS) CANNED CHICKEN OR
   BEEF STOCK
1 CUP FROZEN PEAS
⅓ TSP SALT
½ TSP PEPPER

TOPPING

1 PACKET INSTANT MASH POTATO (PREPARE AS
   SPECIFIED IN PACKAGE INSTRUCTIONS)

1. Heat the oil in a large pan and cook the onion until soft and lightly browned.

2. Add the minced beef and stir, breaking up the meat as it cooks.

3. When well browned, stir in the flour and cook for 2−3 minutes.

4. Add the tomato paste, Worcestershire sauce and herbs. Stir and cook a further 3−4 minutes.

5. Add the stock and bring to a boil, then reduce the heat and cover. Allow it to simmer for 10−15 minutes.

6. Stir in the peas and add salt and pepper to taste. When the peas are heated through and the mixture is quite thick, turn off the heat and set it aside.

7. Preheat the oven to 190°C and prepare the mash potato according to package instructions.

8. Spoon the beef filling into a pie or baking dish 23 cm round or 25 cm by 12 cm rectangle. Spoon the potato over the beef. Rough up or smoothen the surface as preferred.

9. Brush the top with milk or cream and bake for 20 minutes or until the potato is golden and the filling is heated through. Serve immediately.

QUICK CURRY DEVIL

Prep 10 mins | Cook 35 mins | Serves 4

If you know curry devil, you know it's a devilishly time consuming dish. If you know Kristang Eurasians, you know we're mostly a finicky and exacting lot when it comes to our traditional recipes. Still, this will surprise with its authentic flavour, though it's got more shortcuts than the Big Bad Wolf's route to Grandma's house. I came up with this at the request of my eldest, now 18, who is addicted to it and terrified of marrying someone who can't cook this. He wanted a recipe he could easily handle on his own and is pleased as punch with this fiery and flavourful, no-fuss version.

4 TBSP OIL

2 LARGE ONIONS, PEELED AND THINLY SLICED

4 WHOLE CHICKEN LEGS (THIGHS AND DRUMSTICKS STILL ATTACHED TOGETHER) EACH CUT INTO 2 AT THE JOINT

1 TBSP LIGHT SOY SAUCE

4 TSP HOT CHILLI FLAKES (PIRI-PIRI FLAKES ARE WONDERFULLY HOT AND FRAGRANT)

2 TSP GROUND DRIED GINGER

1 TBSP HOT MUSTARD POWDER (PREFERABLY COLMAN'S)

6 SMOKED SAUSAGES, EACH CUT INTO 2 CM LENGTHS

200 ML (1 CUP) WATER

1 TSP SALT

½–1 TSP SUGAR (DON'T GO CRAZY WITH THE SUGAR, CURRY DEVIL IS MEANT TO BE HOTTTTT!)

2 TBSP WHITE VINEGAR

1. Heat the oil in a pot or deep pan and when moderately hot, add the onions and cook, stirring, until limp and beginning to brown.

2. Add the chicken pieces and soy sauce and cook until chicken is browned all over, but take care that the soy sauce doesn't burn.

3. Sprinkle over the chilli, ginger and mustard and stir until the chicken pieces are coated with spices. Take care that the spices don't burn.

4. Add the sausages and stir well to coat with spice mixture. Pour in the water, add salt and sugar and bring to a boil. Stir, then lower heat, cover and simmer for 20 minutes, stirring often to prevent sticking and burning.

5. Add the vinegar, stir and taste. Adjust the seasoning if necessary. Make sure the chicken is not pink or bloody at the bone before turning off the heat.

6. Serve with white rice or slices of baguette.

BAKED CRISPY, SPICY CHICKEN WINGS

Prep 10 mins | Cook 40 mins | Serves 4... ish

You're not going to eat just two or three wings, then happily wash your hands and go away contented, are you? If you're going to have chicken wings, you're going to need at least ten. Don't kid yourself, especially if you're going through the trouble of cooking them yourself; might as well make a few more for your friends. Or for a midnight snack later.

1 KG CHICKEN WINGS, WASHED AND
   DRAINED WELL
1 TBSP TUMERIC POWDER
1½ TBSP CHILLI POWDER (I DID SAY "SPICY")
1½ TSP GARLIC SALT
1 TSP SUGAR
50 G (½ CUP) PLAIN FLOUR

This recipe would work in a tabletop oven but not a toaster oven or pizza toaster. If you're desperate for crispy wings but really don't want to deep-fry them, after rolling the wings in flour and dusting off excess, heat 2 tablespoons oil in a wide and shallow lidded pot, swirl around and heat until hot. Put the chicken wings in one layer and cover the pot. Bring the heat down to a minimum and cook for 12 minutes. Open the lid and turn the pieces over, then cover the pot and cook another 12 – 15 minutes. Test the wings with a fork to make sure there is no blood at the bone. The skin will be crusty and the meat cooked through. Serve immediately. This method works especially well for induction cookers or electric hotplates, and less so for gas stoves and ranges.

1. Preheat the oven at 220°C and line a baking tray with baking parchment.

2. Combine all ingredients, except flour, in a large mixing bowl and mix very thoroughly until the wings are evenly covered in the seasoning.

3. Put the flour in a large plate and spread it out.

4. Roll the wings in the flour one at a time, shake off the excess and arrange them on the baking tray in a single layer.

5. Bake for 20 minutes, then turn the wings over and bake a further 10 minutes.

6. Lower the temperature to 180°C and bake for a final 10 minutes.

7. Remove from the oven and cool slightly before eating.

SAUSAGE AND BAKED BEAN GRATIN

Prep 5 mins | Cook 20 mins | Serves 2

Don't be intimidated by the word "gratin". It's a French cooking term, but all it really means is crusty, cheesy and delicious. This is so easy and quick, you could almost do it with your eyes closed! You don't even need a full-sized oven—a table top model or the kind of toaster oven for heating up a pizza slice would work just fine.

1 CAN BAKED BEANS IN TOMATO SAUCE
4 REGULAR-SIZED SAUSAGES, THICKLY SLICED
45 G (½ CUP) GRATED CHEESE LIKE PARMESAN,
   MOZZARELLA OR A MIXTURE OF BOTH
30 G (½ CUP) PANKO (JAPANESE
   BREADCRUMBS) OR REGULAR
   BREADCRUMBS
1 TSP GARLIC POWDER (OPTIONAL)

1. Preheat the oven at 180°C and combine the baked beans and sausages.

2. Transfer the mixture to a 23 cm by 12 cm baking dish. Smooth the top.

3. Combine the cheese, panko and garlic powder and sprinkle evenly over the bean and sausage mix.

4. Bake for 15–20 minutes or until heated through and the top is bubbly and golden. Serve immediately.

If using a toaster oven, to preheat, turn timer knob to the 30 minutes position and when it reaches 20 minutes, put the dish in.

SIMPLE, PERFECT STEAK

Prep 10 mins | Cook 7 mins | Serves 2

Pan-fried steak may seem too simple a dish to warrant a recipe but getting the perfect doneness is easier said than done. This method guarantees medium rare steak for the given thickness of meat, regardless of weight or size. The term "jus" refers to the pan drippings dissolved with a little liquid. I really feel that good steak should not be cooked beyond medium rare. If you prefer medium steak, add about 1 minute to the overall cooking time. If you want it well-done, add about 3 minutes to the overall cooking time. But please, don't!

2 SIRLOIN OR RIB EYE STEAKS, EACH ABOUT
    2 CM THICK
1 TSP GROUND BLACK PEPPER
½ TSP GARLIC POWDER
¼ TSP SALT
1–2 TBSP VEGETABLE OIL
50 ML (¼ CUP) LIQUID (WATER, WINE,
    LIGHT STOCK OR UNSWEETENED WHITE
    GRAPE JUICE)
½ TBSP WORCESTERSHIRE OR SOY SAUCE
¼ TSP SOFT BROWN SUGAR
1 TBSP BUTTER

1. Rub the steaks well with the pepper, garlic powder and salt.

2. Heat light vegetable oil in a heavy, preferably cast iron frying pan over medium heat, until the pan is very hot.

3. Place the steaks in frying pan. Cook for 1½ minutes on the first side. Turn over and cook the other side for 1½ minutes. If you like them medium rare, do not exceed these timings.

4. Remove the steaks from the pan onto plates (a wire rack is best if you have one) and leave them to relax for 5–10 minutes while you prepare the sauce (gravy or jus).

5. Add the liquid to the pan and stir around, making sure you scrape off the crusty bits on the bottom of the pan.

6. Add the Worcestershire sauce and sugar. Turn the heat up and let the liquid thicken slightly. Add the butter, turn off the heat and stir till the butter melts. Add a little salt to taste, if necessary.

7. Pour the gravy over the steaks and serve immediately with rice, baked or mashed potatoes, shoe string potatoes or French fries.

SAVOURY STEAMED EGGS WITH PORK

Prep 10 mins | Cook 20 mins | Serves 2

I grew up eating tons and tons of this and it always really hit the spot, especially on chilly, rainy days. Vary the ingredients to suit your taste or whatever you have in your kitchen. Cubes of soft tofu are also a lovely addition. Be sure to keep the heat gentle or the eggs will stiffen up and turn rubbery. Ugh!

4 EGGS
200 G MINCED PORK
1 TBSP SESAME OIL
1 TSP SALT
½ TSP PEPPER
1 CAN BUTTON MUSHROOMS, DRAINED
**   AND SLICED**
100 ML (½ CUP) CANNED CHICKEN STOCK
**   OR BROTH**
1 STALK SPRING ONION, WASHED AND SLICED

1. Fill a large wok or deep, wide pot ⅔ full with water and put in an overturned, wide and shallow ceramic bowl.

2. Cover the pot or wok and bring to a boil.

3. Break the eggs into a large bowl or round 20 cm cake tin and beat lightly with a fork.

4. Lightly stir in all the other ingredients until well combined.

5. Lift the cover and gently lower in the bowl with egg mixture.

6. Turn down the heat to a minimum and leave to steam for about 20 minutes or until set (when it feels firm when touched with a clean finger).

7. Turn off the heat and carefully remove the bowl from the wok.

8. Cut or scoop out and serve with rice and sliced chillies in light soy sauce if you like.

SOY SAUCE CHICKEN

Prep 10 mins | Cook 40 mins | Serves 4

Soy sauce chicken is a fixture in Cantonese restaurant menus but is thankfully simple enough to do a good job of at home. The hardest thing about it is waiting for the cooked chicken to cool in the sauce before eating it. This is essential to allow the meat to absorb the sauce, without cooking it to the point of disintegration; good things come to those who wait. I've given generous amounts as any leftovers will taste even better the next day.

100 ML (½ CUP) DARK SOY SAUCE (REGULAR, NOT SWEET)

200 ML (1 CUP) LIGHT SOY SAUCE (PREFERABLY LOW SODIUM)

500 ML (2½ CUPS) WATER

3 TBSP SOFT BROWN SUGAR

1 STICK CINNAMON (ABOUT 5 CM)

1–2 WHOLE STAR ANISE (I LIKE 2 BUT MY BOYS LIKE 1)

5 CM GINGER, PEELED AND BASHED

6 CLOVES GARLIC, BASHED, SKINS DISCARDED

4 WHOLE CHICKEN LEGS (THIGHS AND DRUMSTICKS STILL ATTACHED TOGETHER)

1. Combine all ingredients, except for the chicken, into a medium-sized pot or deep pan and bring mixture to a boil.

2. Add the chicken legs and bring back to a boil, then immediately lower the heat to an absolute minimum. Simmer for about 35 minutes, turning over the pieces every 5 minutes or so to ensure even cooking. If the chicken legs are on the small side, reduce the cooking time to 30 minutes.

3. If the sauce is evaporating too quickly, cover the pot partially, so the sauce won't boil over and spill onto the stove.

4. Turn off the heat after 35 minutes and cover the pot. Allow the chicken to cool off in the sauce.

5. When the chicken is completely cooled, remove it from the sauce and chop it into pieces. Arrange on a platter and spoon the sauce over before serving with white rice, and your favourite garlic chilli dip or sauce.

The chopped up chicken and sauce are superb over blanched noodles, especially broad rice noodles like kway teow. Garnish with shredded spring onions and a dollop of chilli paste or hot chilli flakes.

Store leftovers covered in the fridge. Don't reheat the chicken before eating, as it spoils the flavour of the dish and may toughen the chicken if heated too intensely. Leave the chicken out until it's almost at room temperature, then eat.

Once removed from the fridge, eat all leftovers or just take out the amount you need. The chicken should not be returned to the fridge after being out at room temperature, as this will encourage spoilage.

SIMPLE BEEF RENDANG

Prep 15 mins | Cook 5 hrs | Serves 3

No, you're not seeing things, yes, this is beef rendang and I am telling you that you can easily cook it. Would I lie to you?? There really is nothing much to it, except for lots of coconut milk (sorry, but something's got to give) and hours of gentle simmering while you go about your business. Easiest thing in the world

3 TBSP VEGETABLE OIL

1 LARGE ONION, PEELED, HALVED AND FINELY CHOPPED

1½ TBSP PREPARED GARLIC PASTE

3–4 TBSP PREPARED CHILLI PASTE (GOCHUJANG OR INDONESIAN SAMBAL OELEK)

600 G BEEF (BRISKET, BONELESS SHIN OR SILVERSIDE—ASK THE BUTCHER FOR THESE CUTS AND CUBE IT)

400 ML (2 CUPS) THICK COCONUT MILK

3 STALKS LEMONGRASS, TOP ⅔ TRIMMED OFF, COARSE OUTER LEAVES DISCARDED AND BOTTOMS BASHED

2 TSP SALT

1 TSP SUGAR

SQUEEZE OF LIME JUICE (JUST ENOUGH TO CUT THROUGH RICHNESS OF COCONUT MILK WITHOUT OBVIOUS SOURNESS)

1. If you cannot get hold of a butcher, cut the beef into 2 cm cubes.

2. Heat the vegetable oil in a slow cooker set on "High", with the lid on.

3. When hot, cook the onion, garlic and chilli paste, stirring often, until fragrant and the oil seeps out.

4. Add the beef, and stir with the spices for about 5 minutes.

5. Add the coconut milk, lemongrass, salt and sugar and stir well.

6. Bring to a boil and allow to cook until the liquid thickens (about 30 minutes).

7. Cover and bring heat down to "Low", then simmer covered, for about 4 hours or until tender and the gravy is very thick and coats the meat.

8. Add the lime juice and stir through. Dish out and serve with white rice or nasi lemak.

Try your best to get fresh lemongrass as it's much easier to find than makrut leaves, tumeric leaves or Indonesian bay leaves, all of which add that characteristic aroma to authentic rendang. A sufficient amount of fresh lemongrass can convincingly replace these herbs. If you are really hard pressed to find fresh lemongrass, add a very generous handful of fresh Italian or Thai basil leaves along with the lime juice at the end of cooking.

You can cook this on the stove, but it will entail a lot of stirring, stirring, stirring. Hence the slow cooker, which will only require that you stir everything once every hour or so to ensure even cooking.

TOAD IN THE HOLE

Prep 10 mins | Cook 25 mins | Serves 2–3

The British seem to have a very peculiar sense of humour, judging by the way they name their dishes. Fortunately, this is so much more delicious than it sounds and really easy to make. If you're unwilling to do anything more than open packages and stir the batter, you don't have to include the onion but it isn't much trouble and really does add lots of flavour. The sausage ends sticking out of the puffed up batter are the "toads" and if the batter doesn't rise (boo-hoo) then this sadly becomes "frog in the bog". Just follow the instructions, all will be well

4 TBSP VEGETABLE OIL

1 LARGE ONION, PEELED, HALVED AND THICKLY
    SLICED, THEN BROKEN UP INTO INDIVIDUAL
    HALF RINGS

6 LARGE SAUSAGES (A LITTLE CHUNKY TEXTURE
    IS NICE HERE)

150 G (1½ CUPS) INSTANT PANCAKE MIX
    (BETTY CROCKER GIVES EXCELLENT RESULTS,
    IF YOU CAN FIND IT)

1 TSP GARLIC SALT

½ TSP BLACK PEPPER

250 ML (1¼ CUPS) WATER OR MILK

1. Preheat the oven at 210°C.

2. Put the vegetable oil in a 25 cm by 12 cm rectangular baking dish, and swirl around to evenly coat the bottom and sides.

3. Arrange the onion and sausages in an even layer in the dish and when the oven is hot, bake for 10 minutes or until the sausages and onions are golden.

4. While the sausages bake, stir up the pancake batter with the garlic, salt, pepper and liquid according to the package instructions. **Do not beat batter or over mix**.

5. Open the oven door and pour the batter evenly over the sausages and onions.

6. Quickly close the door and continue to bake another 15 minutes or until the batter is puffed up around the sausages and golden.

7. Test for doneness by sticking a thin, sharp knife into the middle of the baked batter. If the knife comes out clean, remove the dish from the oven.

8. Cut out pieces, including some sausage in each portion and serve immediately.

For a convenient all-in-one meal, add quartered large mushrooms (as much as you like) to the baking dish with the sausages and onions before baking.

Add ½ teaspoon dried mixed herbs to the batter, along with the other seasonings for more flavour.

Add ½ teaspoon dry mustard powder (Colman's Mustard) to the batter along with the other seasonings for a very British flavour accent. Use either the mixed herbs or mustard powder as including both may result in an overpowering flavour.

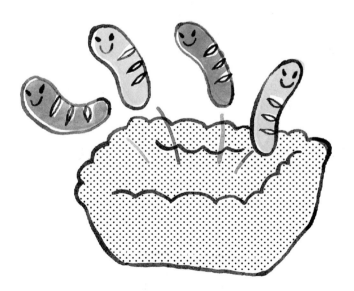

VEGETABLES AND OTHER MEATLESS DISHES

CHAP CHYE

Prep 15 mins | Cook 15 mins | Serves 2–3

I know it doesn't have ten types of vegetables in it, which is cheating since "chap chye" does mean ten vegetables. But this dish is scrumptious even if you're not big on veggies. What you have here is a profusion of rich, savoury flavours and delightfully contrasting textures, but because of the prevalent autumnal shades of this dish, I have to admit it doesn't look striking, or particularly inviting. Just take a leap of faith and trust me when I tell you that if you think you hate vegetables, this dish may just change your mind.

VEGETABLE OIL (3 CM IN THE PAN)

1 SQUARE FIRM TOFU (TAU KUA), CUT INTO
    2 PIECES

4 CLOVES GARLIC, BASHED, SKINS DISCARDED
    AND ROUGHLY CHOPPED

A GENEROUS TBSP VERY SMALL DRIED
    SHRIMPS, RINSED AND DRAINED (OPTIONAL)

½ TSP PEPPER

1½ TBSP TAU CHEO (FERMENTED SOY BEAN
    PASTE) OR JAPANESE MISO

¼ SMALL ROUND CABBAGE, HARD CORE CUT
    OFF, HALVED WIDTH WISE, WASHED AND
    LEAVES SEPARATED

6 FRESH SHIITAKE MUSHROOMS, STEMMED
    AND THICKLY SLICED

1 TSP SUGAR

½ TSP SALT (OR TO TASTE—BE CAREFUL AS THE
    DRIED SHRIMPS AND TAU CHEO GIVE LOTS
    OF FLAVOUR)

1 STALK SPRING ONION, WASHED AND CUT
    INTO 3 CM LENGTHS

1. Heat the oil in a small pan and when hot, fry the tofu halves until quite crisp but not hard.

2. Remove and drain on kitchen paper. When the tofu has cooled, cut across each half into thick slices.

3. Remove most of the oil from the pan (leave behind 3 tablespoons) and fry the garlic, shrimps, pepper and tau cheo until fragrant.

4. Add the cabbage and mushrooms and stir to coat in the tau cheo mixture.

5. Add the tofu, sugar, salt and spring onion. Mix well but gently so tofu doesn't break.

6. Taste and adjust the seasoning if necessary. You probably won't need to add water but if the vegetables seem dry, add 1–2 tablespoons water and stir through.

7. Turn off the heat before the spring onions turn yellow and dish out.

INDIAN STYLE SPINACH STIR-FRY

Prep 15 mins | Cook 10 mins | Serves 2

I recommend spinach because it's so easily available and fresh or frozen will give pretty much the same results. This recipe will also work very well with white Chinese radish slices (daikon), peeled pumpkin cubes or slices, peeled potato cubes or slices, sliced brinjal (eggplant/ aubergine) or sliced lady's fingers (okra).

3 TBSP VEGETABLE OIL

1 TSP BROWN OR DARK WHOLE MUSTARD SEEDS

1 SMALL ONION, PEELED, HALVED AND THINLY
   SLICED

2 SMALL GREEN CHILLIES, THINLY SLICED

3 CLOVES GARLIC, BASHED, SKINS DISCARDED
   AND ROUGHLY CHOPPED

450 G FRESH SPINACH OR 300 G THAWED AND
   SQUEEZED FROZEN SPINACH (SEE TIPS)

1 TSP SALT

1. Heat the vegetable oil in a large pan or wok and when hot, add the mustard seeds.

2. Stir until the seeds start to pop, take care that they don't burn.

3. Add the onion, green chillies and garlic and stir over medium heat until fragrant.

4. Add the spinach stems and cook for about 3 minutes until quite tender.

5. Add the spinach leaves and salt. Stir well until the leaves turn dark green and tender. Dish out and serve immediately.

If using fresh spinach, cut off the roots and 2 cm off the base of the stems close to the roots. Submerge in water and soak for 5 minutes to dislodge grit and soil, if any. Drain and wash a few times until there is no more grit in the water. Pluck off the leaves and snap off the tender parts of stems—the stems will toughen as you get closer to the bottom. Discard any that are too stiff to snap off easily. As you snap off bits of stem, a thin membrane will start to peel off. Pull off these membranes and discard. Separate the stems and leaves and drain very well.

Frozen spinach usually consists of leaves only. Follow thawing instructions and squeeze out as much liquid as you possibly can, then proceed according to the recipe.

SIMPLE TAHU GORENG

CRISP FRIED TOFU IN SPICY PEANUT SAUCE

Prep 10 mins | Cook 5 mins | Serves 2

Don't just reach for a bag of potato crisps or taco chips the next time an anxiety induced snack attack sneaks up on you. Pottering around in the kitchen is a great stress reliever with a built-in reward—a tasty snack that is way better than a greasy, additive laden bag of chips!

VEGETABLE OIL (3 CM IN THE PAN)

4 SMALL SQUARES FIRM TOFU (TAU KUA),
   DRAINED WELL ON KITCHEN PAPER

½ SMALL CUCUMBER, THICKLY SLICED

100 ML (½ CUP) OF YOUR FAVOURITE CHUNKY,
   GARLICKY, SWEET CHILLI SAUCE

AS MUCH COARSELY CRUSHED, READY ROASTED
   PEANUTS AS YOU LIKE

1. Heat vegetable oil in a medium-sized deep pan until hot but not smoking.

2. Carefully lower in the tofu squares and fry on both sides until golden and crisp.

3. Remove the tofu from the pan and drain on kitchen paper.

4. Divide the cucumber slices between two plates, laying them in an even layer.

5. Put two tofu squares on each plate and cut each square into 9 cubes.

6. Top the tofu with the chilli sauce and sprinkle generously with crushed peanuts before serving.

> You can also buy commercial satay sauce in supermarkets and pour it over the tofu instead of the chilli sauce, if preferred. Alternatively, try making your own simple satay sauce (page 82).

SAYUR LODEH
VEGETABLES IN COCONUT MILK
Prep 20 mins | Cook 15 mins | Serves 2–3

This is one vegetable dish which even vegetable haters seem to warm to. Little wonder when vegetables are bathed in creamy coconut milk scented with beautifully tangy lemongrass that is further bolstered with the sweetness of prawns. Crisp fried tumeric flavoured chicken never had a better friend.

4 TBSP OIL

3 CLOVES GARLIC, BASHED, SKINS DISCARDED
AND ROUGHLY CHOPPED

1 SMALL TO MEDIUM ONION, PEELED AND
THINLY SLICED

2 STALKS LEMONGRASS, TOP ⅔ TRIMMED OFF,
COARSE OUTER LEAVES DISCARDED AND
BOTTOMS BASHED

3 RED CHILLIES, SLICED

½ TSP TUMERIC POWDER

400 ML (2 CUPS) WATER

100 G LONG BEANS, TOP AND BOTTOM
DISCARDED AND CUT INTO 4 CM LENGTHS

¼ SMALL ROUND CABBAGE, CUT INTO
SMALL PIECES

1 SMALL EGGPLANT, TOP DISCARDED,
QUARTERED DOWN ITS LENGTH AND
EACH QUARTER CUT INTO 4 CM LENGTHS

100 G PRAWNS, SHELLED

2 SMALL SQUARES FIRM TOFU (TAU KUA),
EACH CUT INTO 2 TRIANGLES AND LIGHTLY
FRIED IN A LITTLE OIL, THEN DRAINED

100 ML (½ CUP) THICK COCONUT MILK

1½ TSP SALT

½ TSP SUGAR

1. Heat the oil in a pot and when moderately hot, add the garlic, onion, lemongrass, chillies and tumeric powder. Stir until fragrant and limp.

2. Add water and bring to a boil. Add the long beans and simmer for about 5 minutes before adding the rest of the vegetables.

3. When the vegetables are tender, add the prawns, tofu pieces and coconut milk. Bring to a boil, then lower heat and simmer to ensure that the prawns and coconut milk are cooked.

4. Season to taste, then turn off the heat. Serve with steamed white rice and spicy fried fish or chicken.

Baby corn, fiddle heads (edible fern shoots) turnips and even small, tender oyster mushrooms are also delicious cooked this way.

Anything cooked with coconut milk must be handled with extra care as coconut milk spoils and sours very easily, especially in warm and humid weather. Cool leftovers rapidly and refrigerate immediately in a clean, covered container. Avoid direct contact with hands and saliva as both harbour lots of bacteria which will make the coconut milk spoil quickly. This means different spoons for eating and scooping up from the communal or serving bowl.

SAMBAL KANG KONG

Prep 15 mins | Cook 10 mins | Serves 2

Kang kong, also known as "ong choy" in Cantonese, water convolvulus, or water spinach, is not as uncommon out of Southeast Asia as it used to be. However, if you do have any trouble tracking it down, tender, young spinach, sweet lettuces like little gem or even strong tasting watercress tops are all very good in their own way.

3 TBSP VEGETABLE OIL

1 VERY SMALL ONION, PEELED, HALVED AND
    THINLY SLICED

3 CLOVES GARLIC, BASHED, SKINS DISCARDED
    AND ROUGHLY CHOPPED

2 TBSP PREPARED CHILLI PASTE

2 TSP FISH SAUCE

⅓ TSP SUGAR

400 G KANG KONG, DAMAGED OR YELLOWED
    LEAVES DISCARDED, AND ONLY YOUNG
    TENDER PARTS OF THE STEMS KEPT

⅓ TSP SALT (OR TO TASTE—BE CAREFUL AS
    FISH SAUCE IS SALTY)

1. Snap off short lengths of kang kong, wash thoroughly and drain very well in colander.

2. Heat the vegetable oil in a deep pan or wok.

3. When hot, fry the onion until soft.

4. Add the garlic, chilli paste, fish sauce and sugar and fry until the oil seeps out.

5. Add the drained kang kong and stir over high heat until coated with the spice mix.

6. Taste and adjust seasoning if necessary.

7. Turn off the heat before the kang kong yellows and dish out immediately.

SPICY CHICKPEAS AND TOMATOES

Prep 5 mins | Cook 20 mins | Serves 2

You're probably tired of hearing your mum telling you to eat your vegetables, but you know, you really should. Fresh leafy greens are my first choice but if you fight shy of cleaning vegetables (wash, wash, wash), here's a painless and delicious way to get what you need, so when mum calls and asks, you can truthfully tell her you've been good!

4 TBSP VEGETABLE OIL

1 TSP CUMIN SEEDS

1 MEDIUM ONION, PEELED, HALVED AND THINLY SLICED

3 CLOVES GARLIC, BASHED, SKINS DISCARDED AND ROUGHLY CHOPPED

2 GREEN CHILLIES, THINLY SLICED

1 CAN COOKED CHICKPEAS, DRAINED

1 CAN DICED TOMATOES WITH JUICE

1 TSP SALT

1. Heat the vegetable oil in a pan until hot but not smoking.

2. Add the cumin seeds and stir until they start to pop, taking care that they don't burn.

3. Add the onion, garlic and green chillies and stir often, until fragrant and soft.

4. Pour in the drained chickpeas, undrained tomatoes and salt, and stir well.

5. Bring to a boil, then reduce heat and simmer until the tomato juices have thickened.

6. Turn off the heat, dish out and serve with rice, chapatti, flat bread or baguette.

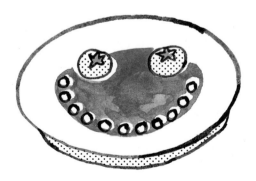

STIR-FRIED BITTER GOURD WITH SALTED BLACK BEANS AND EGGS

Prep 10 mins | Cook 15 mins | Serves 2

You may find this being sold as "bitter melon". Choose one that has wide ridges and a translucent, pale green, thin skin with no hint of yellow. Darker green ones with narrow ridges will taste really bitter. Yellow green skin means it's "old" and will be fibrous. Bittergourd is believed to cleanse the blood and kidneys and cool overheated systems. It has such a reputation as an Asian "health food" that many often overlook how delicious a vegetable it is. You and I, we know better.

1 BITTER GOURD, HALVED LENGTHWISE,
   SEEDS AND WHITE STUFF SCOOPED OUT
   AND DISCARDED
3–4 TBSP VEGETABLE OIL
3 CLOVES GARLIC, BASHED, SKINS DISCARDED
   AND ROUGHLY CHOPPED
1 TBSP BLACK BEAN PASTE (BE CAREFUL
   WITH THIS—IT'S SALTY!)
1 LARGE EGG
PINCH OF SALT

1. Thinly slice off the top and bottom of each bitter gourd half and slice across thinly into half circles.

2. Heat the vegetable oil in a pan or wok and fry the garlic and black bean paste until fragrant and slightly crisp.

3. Add the bitter gourd slices and stir until coated with the black bean and garlic.

4. Continue to stir and cook until the bitter gourd is almost tender.

5. Lightly beat the egg and pour it evenly over the bitter gourd in the pan.

6. Wait a few seconds, then stir to break up the egg.

7. Taste and add a pinch of salt if needed, then turn off the heat and dish out.

You can reduce the bitterness in bitter gourd by rubbing the slices with 2 teaspoons salt, gently so as not to break up the slices. Leave to soak for 5 minutes, then squeeze out the juice from the bitter gourd slices and rinse out the salt in several changes of water. Squeeze dry and proceed according to recipe. I find this step unnecessary if you have chosen your bitter gourd, as described above.

Black bean paste is not the same as tau cheo, which is salted and fermented white soy beans.

Black bean paste is salted fermented black soy beans, and often with garlic added. They taste quite different but for this recipe, the two are interchangeable. Personally I prefer black beans here.

EASY CUCUMBER AND PINEAPPLE ACHAR

Prep 10 mins | Makes 2 cups

The best thing about a very simple achar like this is that it goes with so many dishes like briyani (page 94), nasi lemak (page 93), fried rice, chicken rice (page 96), luncheon meat and mushroom rice (page 97) or fried noodles. It also beautifully perks up simple fried fish or chicken.

1 SMALL CUCUMBER, TOP AND BOTTOM BITS
    DISCARDED, HALVED DOWN ITS LENGTH
    AND THICKLY SLICED
1 RED CHILLI, THICKLY SLICED
½ SMALL VERY RIPE, READY PEELED
    PINEAPPLE, HALVED AGAIN DOWN ITS
    LENGTH AND THICKLY SLICED
100 ML (½ CUP) CHUNKY STYLE SWEET AND
    SOUR GARLIC CHILLI SAUCE
1 TBSP TOASTED SESAME SEEDS

1. Combine all ingredients in a bowl and stir thoroughly.

2. Cover and chill an hour before serving for better flavour.

Try to get a very slim, pale green (but not yellowish) cucumber as it will have far fewer seeds than larger, darker green ones.

If you don't feel it's too much trouble, scrape out the seeds before slicing the cucumber. This will prevent the juices in the soft pulpy flesh surrounding the seeds from leaching out and diluting the flavour of the achar.

Ripe pineapples are very deep yellow and very fragrant.

Adjust the flavour of the achar by adding vinegar and sugar in small amounts until you get the taste you like.

If sesame seeds are unavailable, use crushed roasted peanuts.

Leftovers, if any, should be stored in a clean and dry covered container in the fridge and consumed within 4–5 days.

STIR-FRIED ASIAN GREENS

Prep 15 mins | Cook 3 mins | Serves 2

I'm sorry, but you knew you were going to see this sooner or later. I'm a Mum too. So, here it comes: EAT YOUR VEGETABLES!!

2 TBSP VEGETABLE OIL

3 SLICES GINGER, PEELED AND LIGHTLY BASHED

3 CLOVES GARLIC, BASHED, SKINS DISCARDED AND ROUGHLY CHOPPED

300 G ASIAN GREENS (KAI LAN, BOK CHOY, CHOY SUM, ETC.) (SEE TIPS FOR PREPARATION)

2 TBSP LIGHT SOY SAUCE

DRIZZLE OF SESAME OIL

1. Heat the vegetable oil in a wok or deep pan until really hot.

2. Fry the ginger briefly before adding the garlic and stir around until fragrant. Don't let the garlic burn.

3. Add the vegetables and soy sauce and stir and toss around very quickly until the colour of vegetables deepen. This will take barely 3 minutes.

4. Turn off the heat, add dash of sesame oil, stir and immediately dish out.

Cut off the roots from the vegetables if still attached and submerge the vegetables in water for 5 minutes. Drain and rinse thoroughly in running water. Cut the vegetables into short lengths (length of your pinky) and drain thoroughly in colander.

Leafy vegetables, especially, should always be soaked for a while to effectively remove chemicals from fertilisers and insecticides, even if they are sold as "organic", because honestly, you didn't grow them yourself, so there's no way you'll know with certainty if they're truly as organic as their pretty labels claim. Don't skip the rinsing, to really finish the job.

STIR-FRIED GARLIC FLOWERS WITH TOFU

Prep 15 mins | Cook 10 mins | Serves 2–3

Garlic flowers or ku chai huay are known as garlic scapes in the West and are in abundance in spring. Take advantage of the short season as they are incredibly delicious and even if you think you're all thumbs in the kitchen, they're so jam packed with flavour, even the most challenged of cooks can coax a tasty meal out of them without difficulty.

300 G GARLIC FLOWERS, WASHED AND
    DRAINED
1 SQUARE FIRM TOFU, CUT INTO MEDIUM
    SIZED CUBES
2 CLOVES GARLIC, PEELED AND CHOPPED
1 TBSP LIGHT SOY SAUCE
⅓ TSP SUGAR
¼ TSP WHITE PEPPER
PINCH OF SALT (OPTIONAL)

1. Discard the flower bud at the tip of each garlic flower stalk. Starting from the top of the stalk, break off 2–3 cm lengths, peeling off and discarding any fibres that come off the stalk.

2. Heat enough oil in a pan for shallow frying and when hot, fry the tofu cubes until lightly golden. Remove from the pan, draining off as much oil as possible and place on layers of kitchen paper.

3. Remove most of the oil from the pan, leaving behind about 2 tablespoons oil. When hot, fry the garlic until it is lightly golden and fragrant.

4. Add the garlic flower stems and stir over high heat until they turn a deep green. Add the tofu cubes, soy sauce, sugar and pepper and stir thoroughly but gently, so that the tofu cubes don't break.

5. Taste and add salt if necessary. Turn off the heat and dish out. Serve immediately with rice or porridge.

NOODLES AND PASTA

BAK CHOR MEE

CHAR KWAY TEOW

MEE SIAM

MEE SOTO

FRIED HOKKIEN MEE

MACARONI AND CHEESE

FRIED BEE HOON

CHAR MEE

ONE POT TOMATO AND CORNED BEEF
 MACARONI

SATAY BEE HOON

BEE TAI BAK IN GREEN TEA

PRAWN NOODLE SOUP

NOODLE SOUP WITH CHICKEN AND CHINESE
 GREENS

CHAR SIEW AND DUMPLING NOODLES

BAK CHOR MEE

Prep 10 mins | Cook 10 mins | Serves 1

This is the ultimate comfort food for many Singaporeans. There's nothing quite like the combination of succulent minced meat, tender noodles and chilli spiked oil to soothe the frazzled soul and satisfy the hungry stomach. Asian flavoured oils should be available in most countries, but if they aren't, making them is not difficult at all, and having these fragrant oils in the kitchen is a great boon to stirring up quick, easy and delicious meals, like spicy pasta, soups, flavoured rice or stir fries, at the drop of a hat.

150–200 G MINCED PORK (COARSELY MINCED, IF YOU CAN FIND IT)
1 TSP GARLIC SALT OR GARLIC POWDER (USE REGULAR SALT IF YOU CAN'T FIND EITHER)
1 TBSP SESAME OIL
3 TBSP WATER
½ TSP PEPPER
1 COIL OR SQUARE DRIED FLAT EGG NOODLES
1–2 TBSP CHILLI GARLIC OIL (SEE TIPS FOR RECIPE)
1 TBSP LIGHT SOY SAUCE
AS MUCH SLICED SPRING ONIONS AS YOU LIKE, TO GARNISH

1. Bring a small pot of water to a boil.

2. In a large microwave safe bowl, combine the pork, garlic salt or powder, sesame oil, water and pepper and stir until well mixed.

3. Cover the bowl and microwave on "High" for 2 minutes. Remove and stir to break up any lumps.

4. Microwave again on "High" for 1 minute. The pork should be cooked and no longer pink in colour. Break up any lumps, cover and keep aside.

5. When the water boils, cook the noodles according to package instructions, ensuring the noodles are not overcooked.

6. Put the chilli garlic oil and soy sauce into a deep bowl. Drain the noodles and put into bowl with oil and soy sauce.

7. Stir the noodles well and top with the minced meat. Garnish with spring onions and serve immediately.

If you can't find dried flat egg noodles, use the noodle cake from a packet of instant mee pok noodles or try using slightly overcooked and drained linguine or fettuccine.

To make **chilli garlic oil** for dressing noodles, combine 2 tablespoons finely chopped garlic or garlic paste, 2 tablespoons dried chilli or hot red pepper flakes, 1 teaspoon salt and 1 cup vegetable oil in a microwave safe bowl and cook on "Low" for 10 minutes or until oil is deep red and very fragrant. Alternatively, combine everything in a small pot or pan and cook over very low heat on the stove until the oil is deep red and fragrant. Cool the oil and store covered at room temperature. Use within a week.

CHAR KWAY TEOW

Prep 20 mins | Cook 15 mins | Serves 2–3

Char kway teow is often cited as one of the local dishes most craved by homesick Singaporeans; perfectly understandable to anyone who has tasted it. I pre-fry the noodles over as furious a heat as a domestic stove can achieve, to capture that wondrously smoky but elusive (in home cooking) essence of wok frying done right, known as "wok hei" which means air or fragrance of the wok. This can only be achieved with fierce heat, so go ahead, act out all your latent pyromaniac fantasies while cooking dinner; just be sure to turn on the cooker hood before you start.

6 TBSP OIL

6 CLOVES GARLIC, PEELED AND CHOPPED

300 G FRESH KWAY TEOW (BROAD RICE
    NOODLES), LOOSENED

4 TBSP LIGHT SOY SAUCE

1 TBSP PREPARED CHILLI PASTE

100 G PRAWNS, SHELLED

2 CHINESE OR JAPANESE FRIED FISH CAKES,
    THINLY SLICED

2 EGGS

60 G BEAN SPROUTS, RINSED AND DRAINED

A SMALL HANDFUL FLAT CHINESE CHIVES,
    FIBROUS BOTTOMS DISCARDED, AND CUT
    INTO 3 CM LENGTHS

70 ML (⅓ CUP) WATER

1. Heat about 3 tablespoons of oil in a wok or deep pan until very hot. Add half the garlic and stir very quickly before adding the kway teow.

2. Stir and toss over very high heat, then drizzle over 3 tablespoons of the soy sauce. Stir and continue to cook until the kway teow is charred in parts and smells smoky. Remove from the pan and set aside.

3. Add 3 tablespoons of oil to the pan and over high heat, fry the remaining garlic quickly so it doesn't burn. Add the chilli paste and stir-fry until fragrant and your nose tingles.

4. Add the prawns and fish cake and stir-fry again until prawns change colour.

5. Break in the eggs and scramble with the other ingredients. Return the kway teow to the pan and mix everything together. Keep the heat high and continue to cook for 2–3 minutes or until a smoky scent emerges.

6. Add the vegetables and stir through the noodles. Quickly sprinkle the water over everything and stir and turn the mixture until most of the liquid evaporates but the noodles are still slightly shiny and slick and the vegetables remain crisp.

7. Dish out and serve immediately.

MEE SIAM

Prep 20 mins | Cook 40 mins | Serves 4

Mee siam means Siamese noodles in Malay and holds many happy childhood memories for me. I ate it several times a week when I was a wee girl in school. It was very simple, the way the school canteen lady made it, with just some fried tofu cubes, sprouts and a spare sprinkling of chives. At that time, unknown to my mother and grandmother, I preferred this bare bones version to their elaborate ones. But my tastes have since "grown up" and these days, I prefer my mee siam more nicely fleshed out, thank you.

100 ML (½ CUP) OIL

2 SMALL SQUARES FIRM TOFU (TAU KUA) CUT INTO SMALL RECTANGLES (ABOUT STAMP SIZE) AND DRAINED

1 LARGE ONION, PEELED AND CHOPPED

6 CLOVES GARLIC, PEELED AND CHOPPED

1 TBSP GRANULATED BELACAN OR ANCHOVY SOUP POWDER

5 TBSP PREPARED CHILLI PASTE

3 TBSP TAU CHEO (FERMENTED SOY BEAN PASTE) OR JAPANESE MISO

1½ TSP SALT (SEASON CAREFULLY AS BELACAN AND TAU CHEO ARE BOTH SALTY)

400 G BEE HOON, SOAKED AND THOROUGHLY DRAINED

100 G BEAN SPROUTS, WASHED AND DRAINED

400 G SMALL TO MEDIUM PRAWNS, SHELLED

800 ML (5 CUPS) WATER

3 SLICES TAMARIND

1 TBSP SUGAR

1 HANDFUL FLAT CHINESE CHIVES, FIBROUS BOTTOMS DISCARDED, AND CUT INTO 1 CM LENGTHS

CALAMANSI LIME HALVES, TO GARNISH

BOILED EGG HALVES, TO GARNISH (OPTIONAL)

1. Heat the oil in a deep pan and when moderately hot, fry the drained tofu pieces until golden and lightly crisp. Remove from the pan and drain on kitchen paper.

2. Remove about ⅓ of the oil from the pan and heat again until moderately hot.

3. Add the chopped onion, garlic and belacan and stir for about 5 minutes, before adding the chilli paste, tau cheo and salt. Continue to cook, stirring often, until fragrant and the spices separate from the oil.

4. Remove about ⅓ of the spice paste and transfer to a medium pot for later use.

5. Add the bee hoon to the spices in the pan and stir and toss thoroughly until coated with the spices. Add the bean sprouts and stir through bee hoon. Add a little water to the bee hoon if it sticks to the pan and stir through to loosen the bee hoon. Turn off heat and set aside.

6. Heat the pot with the spice mixture in it and add the prawns. Stir until the prawns change colour.

7. Add the water, tamarind slices and sugar and bring to a boil. Lower the heat and simmer until the gravy is as tart as you like. The longer you simmer, the more the sourness will seep out of the tamarind. Taste and adjust the seasoning if necessary.

8. To serve, put some bee hoon in a deep plate and ladle as much gravy as you like. Garnish with tofu, chives, lime and egg and serve immediately.

For perfect boiled eggs, bring a pot of water to a boil, then lower heat to a simmer before lowering the eggs in gently with a spoon. Bring the heat back up slightly so the eggs boil gently. Cook for 11 minutes (time it) then remove eggs and soak in water to cool off. Roll the eggs on a clean surface until the shells are covered in cracks and ease off the shells. Rinse eggs and cut in half with a sharp knife or a length of thread or dental floss.

The eggs should be at room temperature when you put them into the pot or they won't be fully cooked at the centre.

MEE SOTO

INDONESIAN SPICY CHICKEN SOUP WITH NOODLES

Prep 20 mins | Cook 40 mins | Serves 2

Remember that sup ayam a few pages back? I like my recipes to work harder for you, so here's something else scrumptious and oh, so satisfying that you can do with it.

1 RECIPE SUP AYAM (PAGE 24)—OMIT THE
  POTATO AND CARROT IF YOU WISH
300 G HOKKIEN NOODLES
60 G BEAN SPROUTS
AS MUCH CHILLI GARLIC OIL AS YOU LIKE
  (PAGE 72)
1 STALK CHINESE CELERY OR THE LEAFY TOPS
  OF REGULAR CELERY, WASHED, DRAINED
  AND CUT INTO SHORT LENGTHS
READY FRIED CRISP SHALLOTS, TO GARNISH
2 LIME QUARTERS

1. Cook the sup ayam and remove the chicken pieces when cooked. Keep it covered and simmering.

2. Put a deep pot of water to boil.

3. When the chicken pieces have cooled, discard the skins, shred the meat and set aside. Discard the bones.

4. When the water boils, blanch half the noodles by putting in a noodle basket and plunging in the boiling water. Keep the noodles moving in the water for 30 seconds, then drain and put in a deep plate.

5. Next, plunge half the bean sprouts in the hot water for about 30 seconds, then put them on top of the noodles.

6. Repeat with the remaining noodles and sprouts for the other serving.

7. Top each plate of noodles with some shredded chicken.

8. Ladle the very hot soup over both plates until the noodles are submerged.

9. Top each serving with some of the chilli and garlic solids from the chilli garlic oil, a sprinkling of celery and crisp shallots.

10. Squeeze a quarter of lime over each serving and eat.

FRIED HOKKIEN MEE

Prep 20 mins | Cook 15 mins | Serves 2

A "full dress" version would include fresh squid slices, boiled belly pork strips and bee hoon as well as Hokkien noodles. It seems the fascinatingly grotesque squid strikes fear into not only timid eaters but less stout-hearted cooks too. As fresh, cleaned squid is hard to come by, I've excluded it, along with bee hoon, which seems rare in most parts of the west and pork belly, which though delicious, gives many the heebie-jeebies thanks to its impressive cholesterol and fat levels. No worries, this is still so good, it's positively wicked!

4–5 TBSP OIL

4 CLOVES GARLIC, PEELED AND CHOPPED

100 G BONELESS CHICKEN MEAT OR PORK
FILLET, THINLY SLICED

150 G PRAWNS, SHELLED

1–2 EGGS

300 G FRESH HOKKIEN NOODLES

1 TBSP LIGHT SOY SAUCE

1 TBSP DARK SOY SAUCE

½–1 TSP SALT

½ TSP SUGAR

1–1½ CUPS CHICKEN STOCK

A SMALL HANDFUL FLAT CHINESE CHIVES,
FIBROUS BOTTOMS DISCARDED, WASHED,
DRAINED AND CUT INTO 3 CM LENGTHS

30 G BEAN SPROUTS

1. Heat the oil in a large pan or wok and when moderately hot, fry the garlic until fragrant and light brown.

2. Turn up the heat to maximum and add the chicken or pork and stir well until it changes colour.

3. Add the prawns and cook, stirring often, until they change colour.

4. Break in the egg(s) and scramble with the rest of the ingredients in the pan.

5. Add the noodles and stir-fry while cutting the noodles until they begin to brown and smell smoky.

6. Add the soy sauces, salt, sugar and stock, stir well and bring to a boil. Cover the pan or wok and allow everything to steam together for about 3 minutes, so that the flavours mingle and permeate the noodles.

7. Remove the cover and stir in the chives and sprouts for about a minute. Don't overcook.

8. Dish out the noodles and serve with sambal, chilli garlic oil (page 72) or sliced red chillies in light soy sauce and calamansi lime halves.

MACARONI AND CHEESE

Prep 10 mins | Cook 25 mins | Serves 4

I know too much cheese spells trouble for your bikini, or skinny jeans, but, IF you want to do something wrong, do it right! There's enough cheese here to make even the Greeks or French blush, but as my boy says, if I have to ask "Where's the cheese?"… it's not mac and cheese! Eat this when summer's over and hide your indiscretions under your autumn or winter layers; you're purring in sweet contentment, and no one is any the wiser.

350 G SHORT PASTA (MACARONI, SHELLS, SPIRALS OR PENNE)

2 CANS CAMPBELL'S CONDENSED CREAM OF CHICKEN SOUP

300 ML (1½ CUPS) WATER

100 G (1 SLIGHTLY ROUNDED CUP) GRATED CHEDDAR OR GOUDA CHEESE

2 TSP PREPARED ENGLISH MUSTARD— COLMAN'S OR GRAINY FRENCH MUSTARD (GIVES A NICE BITE)

½–1 TSP SALT

½ TSP GROUND WHITE PEPPER

100 ML (½ CUP) CREAM OR SOUR CREAM (I LIKE SOUR CREAM)

100 G (1 SLIGHTLY ROUNDED CUP) GRATED PARMESAN CHEESE (FRESHLY GRATED PREFERRED)

50 G (½ CUP) PANKO (JAPANESE BREADCRUMBS) OR REGULAR BREADCRUMBS

1. Preheat oven at 230°C.

2. Bring a deep pot of water to boil, then add the pasta and cook for about 8 minutes. Don't overcook. Keep the water boiling vigorously and stir the pasta to prevent clumping.

3. While the pasta cooks, combine the condensed soup and water in a large pot. Stir with a whisk and bring to a boil. Add in Cheddar or Gouda, lower the heat and whisk until cheese melts. Add mustard, salt and pepper, whisk in and taste sauce. Adjust the seasoning if necessary. When the sauce is smooth, turn off the heat.

4. Drain the pasta thoroughly and add to the sauce in the pot. Pour in the cream and stir thoroughly but gently. Taste again and add salt if necessary.

5. Pour the mixture into a rectangular baking dish, scraping off every bit of sauce from the pot. Level the surface lightly.

6. Combine the Parmesan and breadcrumbs and sprinkle evenly over the pasta. Bake for about 15 minutes or until the top is golden and crusty.

7. Remove the dish from the oven and cool for about 5 minutes before cutting and serving.

FRIED BEE HOON

Prep 20 mins | Cook 15 mins | Serves 2

Bread or bacon and eggs for breakfast is fine, but as an Asian, every now and then I crave a plate of oil-slicked, garlicky, savoury and slightly spicy fried bee hoon for breakfast. There are days when nothing else will hit the spot! Of course, you could always eat this for lunch, dinner or any time you damn well please.

3 TBSP OIL

4 CLOVES GARLIC, PEELED AND CHOPPED

1 TBSP PREPARED CHILLI PASTE

1 LARGE FRIED FISH CAKE, THINLY SLICED

50 G MUSTARD GREENS (OR ANY LEAFY ASIAN GREENS), CUT INTO 5 CM LENGTHS

200 G BEE HOON, SOAKED AND DRAINED

60 G BEAN SPROUTS, WASHED AND DRAINED

2 TBSP LIGHT SOY SAUCE

1 TSP SALT

½ TSP SUGAR

If you don't have a non-stick pan or your pan is not well seasoned, the bee hoon may stick while cooking. If this happens, drizzle about half a cup of hot water evenly over the bee hoon and stir well, scraping the bottom of the pan as you do so, to dislodge stuck on bits. Turn off the fire as soon as the bee hoon comes unstuck. Once the liquid has completely evaporated, the bee hoon will start to stick again.

1. Heat the pan until moderately hot and add oil. Fry the garlic and chilli paste until fragrant, stirring continuously to prevent burning.

2. Add the fish cake and stir until it is coated with the chilli paste.

3. Add the mustard greens and drained bee hoon and stir well, turning and tossing until the bee hoon strands are well coated with chilli paste.

4. Sprinkle the bean sprouts over the noodles and stir in until well mixed with the bee hoon. **Do not overcook**; the mustard greens should still be bright green and the sprouts should have some crunch.

5. Add the soy sauce, salt and sugar and mix thoroughly. Taste and add more seasoning if necessary.

6. Turn off the heat and serve with a saucer of red chilli slices in soy sauce, if you like.

CHAR MEE

Prep 15 mins | Cook 10 mins | Serves 2

Everyone should have a simple fried noodle dish in their repertoire. This one uses easily available ingredients and is lightning quick to put together. The ingredients are only suggestions. Like fried rice, char mee has no real "recipe" and is a really good vehicle for whatever ingredients you have on hand.

4 TBSP VEGETABLE OIL

4 CLOVES GARLIC, BASHED, SKINS DISCARDED AND ROUGHLY CHOPPED

2 CHINESE OR JAPANESE COOKED FISH CAKES, SLICED

300 G FRESH HOKKIEN NOODLES SEPARATED AND CUT OR PULLED INTO SHORTER LENGTHS

2 EGGS

200 G ASIAN GREENS (KAI LAN, BOK CHOY, CHOY SUM, ETC.), ROOT STUMPS DISCARDED AND CUT INTO 5 CM LENGTHS

1 TBSP LIGHT SOY SAUCE

200 ML (1 CUP) LOW FAT CANNED CHICKEN STOCK OR BROTH

Substitute fish cakes with sliced lap cheong (Chinese sausages) or use both for more flavour.

Can't get fresh Hokkien noodles? Use 3 or 4 packs of instant noodles that have been soaked in hot water long enough to untangle them, and thoroughly drained.

A squeeze of lime juice will really lift the taste of this dish.

This dish also goes well with achar (page 67).

1. Heat the oil in a wok or wide and deep pan (like a skillet) until hot but not smoking.

2. Fry the garlic until fragrant, then add the fish cakes and stir until slightly brown.

3. Add the noodles and stir well over high heat until the noodles are lightly charred and smell smoky.

4. Push the noodles to the side of pan or wok and, on the other side, break in the eggs.

5. Allow the eggs to set slightly, then scramble until they are almost cooked through.

6. Combine the eggs and noodles, then add vegetables, soy sauce and stock.

7. Stir well over high heat until most of the stock has evaporated, and the vegetables are still green.

8. Turn off the heat and dish out.

ONE POT TOMATO AND CORNED BEEF MACARONI

Prep 5 mins | Cook 20 mins | Serves 4–6

Cooking pasta usually means two pots to wash up—one for the pasta and one for the sauce. Not cool! This, you cook like rice or risotto, all simmered in one pot until the liquid is absorbed. It makes sense to cook pasta in big amounts as it keeps and reheats well. If possible, pasta tastes even better the next day, so leftovers are a bonus as it means at least one less meal to cook in your busy week! Or, invite your buddies over for an easy, scrumptious and filling meal instead of storing the leftovers for yourself; one way to ensure future requested favours are happily granted.

5 TBSP VEGETABLE OIL

1 LARGE ONION, PEELED, HALVED AND
THINLY SLICED

2 RED CHILLIES, THINLY SLICED

1 CAN TOMATO PUREE

2 TSP COARSELY GROUND BLACK PEPPER

500 G (1 PACK) MACARONI OR ANY STURDY,
SHORT PASTA SHAPE

1.2 L (6 CUPS) WATER

1 CAN CORNED BEEF

PINCH OF SALT

1. Heat the vegetable oil in a wide and deep pot.

2. When the pot is hot but not smoking, fry the onion and chillies until fragrant and transparent.

3. Add tomato puree and stir until it darkens and the oil seeps out before adding the pepper.

4. Add the uncooked macaroni and stir quickly, then pour in the water and stir well.

5. Bring to a boil, then lower the heat to a minimum and cover the pot.

6. After 10 minutes, lift the cover and gently stir the macaroni so that the bottom doesn't burn.

7. Add the corned beef and gently break up, then stir gently through the macaroni until it is well mixed.

8. Cover the pot again and leave it to cook for a final 5–10 minutes to heat through and dry up excess moisture. Season with salt and serving.

Garnish with chopped coriander leaves or spring onions for more colour and visual appeal.
   This method only works well for short pasta shapes like elbow macaroni, penne, fusilli (spirals), farfalle (bow ties), etc. Long pasta like spaghetti, linguine or fettuccine won't give good results as they tend to get tangled and stick together. If you only have long pasta, break them up into short lengths (no more than 3 cm).

SATAY BEE HOON

Prep 15 mins | Cook 10 mins | Serves 2

Satay bee boon is a delectable crossbreed of local Chinese and Malay cuisines. Main ingredients are rice vermicelli, satay sauce, pork slices, kang kong, cured cuttlefish and fresh cockles. Finding some of these ingredients would definitely pose a challenge outside of Southeast Asia, so the version below uses ingredients common to many food cultures or available in decent supermarkets almost anywhere in the world, for a dish that will still bring you a taste of home.

2 SMALL FRIED CHINESE FISH CAKES,
   THICKLY SLICED
2 PACKETS INSTANT RICE VERMICELLI
1 TBSP LIGHT SOY SAUCE
2 TSP SESAME OIL
200 ML (1 CUP) PREPARED SATAY SAUCE
½ SMALL CUCUMBER, SHREDDED OR SLICED
TOASTED SESAME SEEDS, TO GARNISH
   (OPTIONAL)

1. Boil a small pot of water and when boiling, blanch, then drain the fish cakes and leave to cool.

2. While the fish cakes cool, cook the vermicelli briefly in the same pot, according to package instructions.

3. Drain the bee hoon thoroughly into a large bowl and toss well with soy sauce and sesame oil.

4. Divide the bee hoon between 2 plates and top each plate with half the satay sauce.

5. Top each serving with the desired amount of shredded fish cake and cucumber.

6. Garnish with sesame seeds and serve immediately.

Commercially prepared **satay sauce** is available in most supermarkets in the west these days, as satay has become a well known dish. If however you cannot find it, thoroughly combine ⅔ cup chunky peanut butter, 1 generous handful roasted peanuts, finely chopped, 2 teaspoons soft brown sugar, 1 generous squeeze of lime juice, 1 − 2 teaspoon of chilli flakes and ½ teaspoon prepared garlic paste. If mixture is clumpy or too thick, thin down with water a little at a time until sauce is to your preferred consistency.

BEE TAI BAK IN GREEN TEA

Prep 10 mins | Cook 10 mins | Serves 1

This is one of the most popular recipes on my blog, "Quickies on the Dinner Table", and by that virtue, I have decided to include it here. I originally made this to use up leftovers in my fridge, but liked its fresh, bright flavour and Zen sensibility so much, it has become something I make very often in my own kitchen, especially on lazy, lazy, slow-as-dripping-tar days. Sometimes I use leftover fresh noodles, sometimes leftover cooked rice, so feel free to play around with starches, topping ingredients and garnishes.

1 GREEN TEA BAG

1 CUP BEE TAI BAK (SHORT FRESH RICE NOODLES)

8 PRAWNS, BOILED AND SHELLED

2 TBSP LIGHT SOY SAUCE

1 TBSP SLICED SPRING ONIONS

1. Boil a kettle of water.

2. When the water boils, make a cup of tea with the tea bag. Soak for about 4 minutes, then discard bag. Keep the tea hot.

3. Cover the noodles with boiling water and soak for about 3 minutes before draining. Rinse the prawns with hot water and drain.

4. Transfer the noodles to a bowl. Combine the hot tea and soy sauce and pour over the noodles.

5. Top with the spring onions and prawns and serve immediately.

PRAWN NOODLE SOUP

Prep 45 mins | Cook 40 mins | Serves 4

I know you don't want to spend hours in the kitchen, as much as you may love prawn noodles, so I have simplified this as far as possible while retaining the essence of its character. Don't skip frying the prawn shells before simmering for your stock; it makes a world of difference! I've given a recipe for four because if you're going to take the trouble to peel little prawns (you need the shells!) and lovingly simmer stock, you might as well invite some friends over to share the booty.

600 G FRESH HOKKIEN NOODLES
100 G BEAN SPROUTS (OR AS MUCH AS YOU LIKE)
2 FRIED FISH CAKES, THINLY SLICED
READY FRIED CRISP SHALLOTS, TO GARNISH
SLICED RED CHILLIES, TO GARNISH

PRAWN STOCK
24 MEDIUM TO LARGE PRAWNS (MUCH EASIER TO PEEL), RINSED AND DRAINED
2 TBSP OIL
4 CLOVES GARLIC, PEELED AND CHOPPED
2 TBSP TAU CHEO (FERMENTED SOY BEAN PASTE) OR JAPANESE MISO
½ TSP GROUND WHITE PEPPER
1.5 L (7–8 CUPS) WATER
4 TBSP LIGHT SOY SAUCE
2 TSP SALT
2 TSP SUGAR

1. Put the prawns into a pot and pour over enough of the water (from the 1.5 L) to completely cover the prawns. Bring to a boil and when all the prawns change colour completely and the liquid turns frothy (about 2 minutes after water starts boiling), turn off the heat and remove the prawns from pot, saving the boiling liquid.

2. Cool the prawns, then peel off the heads and shells completely. Set the prawns aside and reserve the heads and shells.

3. Heat the oil in a large pot and when moderately hot, fry the garlic and tau cheo until fragrant.

4. Add the prawn heads and shells and pepper to the pot. Stir well for about 3 minutes or until the shells are coated with mixture.

5. Pour in the reserved water from boiling the prawns, the remainder of the 1.5 L of water and soy sauce. Add salt and sugar. Bring to a boil, then lower heat and simmer for 30 minutes.

6. Discard the prawn heads and shells and keep the stock hot. Taste and adjust seasoning if necessary.

7. While the stock is simmering, put another deep pot of water to boil for blanching the noodles.

8. When the water boils, for each serving, blanch a quarter of the noodles briefly (30 seconds maximum) and put into a deep bowl. Briefly blanch some bean sprouts (15 seconds maximum) and lay them on the noodles. Finally, blanch a quarter of the fish cake slices briefly (15 seconds) and add to the bowl of noodles and sprouts.

9. Top each serving with six of the cooked prawns and ladle over enough stock to cover the noodles or as much stock as you like.

10. Garnish with the crisp shallots and sliced chillies and serve immediately.

Don't simmer the stock longer than recommended as it will smell unpleasantly of prawns.

If fresh Hokkien noodles are not available, use one noodle cake (from a packet of instant noodles) per serving and blanch until noodles are hydrated but still springy. Fresh ramen noodles are a good option too.

NOODLE SOUP WITH CHICKEN AND CHINESE GREENS

Prep 10 mins | Cook 10 mins | Serves 2

Preparing this super simple, light and refreshing meal in a bowl takes barely more effort than calling for pizza delivery. It can't be beaten when you're under the weather, fighting a cold, battling the bulge, cramming for finals but need a bolstering break from the books, or just really want to take it easy in the kitchen.

800 ML (4 CUPS) LOW FAT CANNED CHICKEN
    STOCK OR BROTH
2 TBSP LIGHT SOY SAUCE
4 SLICES GINGER, PEELED (OPTIONAL)
2 CHICKEN BREAST HALVES, SKINNED AND
    EACH SLICED ACROSS INTO 6 PIECES
80 G (2 BUNDLES) DRIED RICE STICK NOODLES
    (OR FRESH RICE NOODLES LIKE KWAY TEOW)
100 G ASIAN GREENS (KAI LAN, BOK CHOY, CHOY
    SUM, ETC.), CUT INTO 5 CM LENGTHS
DRIZZLE OF SESAME OIL (OPTIONAL)

1. Combine the stock, soy and ginger in a small pot and bring to a boil.

2. Lower the heat to minimum, add the chicken pieces and cook gently for 3 minutes if using dried noodles, or 5 minutes if using fresh noodles.

3. Increase the heat, add the noodles and cook until noodles are just tender but not mushy.

4. Add the greens and cook only until just tender but still green.

5. Divide the noodles, chicken and greens between two large bowls and ladle over the hot broth.

6. Drizzle with sesame oil before serving.

CHAR SIEW AND DUMPLING NOODLES

Prep 20 mins | Cook 1 hr | Serves 1

Did you think I would teach you how to make something without showing you how to use it, and use it, and use it again?! You wound me, but I forgive you. I know you're going to miss your weekly bowl of wonton mee, so, enjoy!

1 RECIPE CHAR SIEW (PAGE 45)

2 TBSP CHILLI GARLIC OIL (PAGE 72)

1½ TBSP LIGHT SOY SAUCE

2 TBSP HOT WATER (FROM THE NOODLE
    BLANCHING WATER)

1 PORTION UNCOOKED RAMEN NOODLES,
    LOOSENED AND UNTANGLED

6 FROZEN GYOZA (DUMPLINGS OR POT
    STICKERS), THAWED ACCORDING TO
    PACKAGE INSTRUCTIONS

AS MUCH SHREDDED SPRING ONIONS AS
    YOU LIKE

1. Prepare the char siew according to the recipe and when cool, cut off 10–12 thin slices.

2. Put a small deep pot of water to boil.

3. Put the chilli garlic oil (including chilli and garlic solids) and soy sauce into a noodle bowl and mix.

4. Add 2 tablespoons of hot water to the chilli oil mixture and stir until well mixed.

5. When the water boils, blanch the noodles according to package instructions, taking care not to overcook them. Rinse the noodles off in cold water from tap and plunge again, once, into the boiling water.

6. Drain off the water well and put the noodles into chilli oil and soy sauce mix.

7. Stir and toss the noodles gently to coat with oil and soy dressing.

8. Arrange the char siew slices on the noodles.

9. Very briefly blanch the gyoza in the boiling water and place on the noodles, beside the char siew.

10. Garnish with spring onions and serve with an extra dollop of the chilli and garlic solids from the oil.

RICE

CHEESY MUSHROOM AND HAM BAKED RICE

CHILLI CRAB FRIED RICE

NASI LEMAK

EASY PEASY BRIYANI

CHICKEN RICE

LUNCHEON MEAT AND MUSHROOM RICE

TEOCHEW MUAY

CANTONESE STYLE PLAIN RICE PORRIDGE

WHITE RICE

CHEESY MUSHROOM AND HAM BAKED RICE

Prep 15 mins | Cook 35 mins | Serves 3 – 4

Anything covered in cheese and baked in the oven spells comfort food for me. The layer of savoury ham and mushroom studded rice waiting to be scooped out from a blanket of rich, bubbly, molten cheese makes it oh, so much better!

2 TBSP BUTTER

1 TBSP OIL

1 MEDIUM ONION, PEELED AND CHOPPED

200 G MUSHROOMS, DICED INTO LARGE PIECES

8 SLICES HAM, DICED INTO LARGE PIECES

300 G (2 CUPS) UNCOOKED RICE, WASHED
    AND DRAINED

600 ML (3 CUPS) WATER OR CHICKEN STOCK

1 TSP SALT (USE LESS IF YOU'RE USING STOCK
    INSTEAD OF WATER)

1 CAN CAMPBELL'S CONDENSED CREAM OF
    CHICKEN OR MUSHROOM SOUP

AS MUCH GRATED CHEESE AS YOU LIKE
    (A COMBINATION OF MOZZARELLA AND
    CHEDDAR IS NICE)

CHOPPED FRESH PARSLEY LEAVES, TO GARNISH
    (OPTIONAL)

1. Heat the butter and oil together in a heavy based pot over moderate heat until the butter melts. Add the onion, mushrooms and ham and stir around until the onions and mushrooms are limp and the mixture is fragrant.

2. Add the drained rice and stir gently until the rice grains are coated with butter and oil.

3. Pour in the water or stock and salt and stir. Bring to a boil and cook until most of the liquid has evaporated and little holes appear on the surface of the rice. Reduce the heat to a minimum and cover the pot securely.

4. Leave to cook gently for 8 – 10 minutes, then turn off the heat and leave covered for 15 minutes.

5. Preheat oven at 190°C and get four individual baking dishes (disposable individual foil baking trays are convenient) or one large baking dish ready.

6. Gently break up the rice in the pot with a rice paddle (flat scoop) and divide among the four dishes or put everything into the large dish in an even layer.

7. Top the rice with the condensed soup straight from the can. Make sure you cover the rice evenly, right to the edges. Sprinkle as much cheese as you like, as evenly as you can, right to the edges.

If you like a crunchier top, sprinkle the soup topped rice with a mixture of ⅓ panko and ⅔ grated cheese before baking.

8. Bake the rice for about 15 minutes or until cheese is bubbly and golden. Remove from the oven and allow to cool for a few minutes. Garnish with parsley and serve.

CHILLI CRAB FRIED RICE

Prep 15 mins | Cook 15 mins | Serves 2 – 3

You could get canned or frozen crab meat for this but I must honestly tell you that both are usually terribly disappointing, while fresh crab is shockingly expensive and too much of a bother even for me to happily handle, on most days. So, crab flavoured surimi to the rescue. Don't scoff—slightly pricier, better quality surimi crab sticks are quite a decent stand in for the real thing. This simple but lovely fried rice encapsulates the essence of chilli crab without the expense, bother and crabicide associated anguish.

4 TBSP VEGETABLE OIL

1 LARGE ONION, PEELED, HALVED AND SLICED

3 TBSP PREPARED CHILLI PASTE (GOCHUJANG OR TOM YUM PASTE WILL DO TOO)

2 EGGS

250 G GOOD QUALITY SURIMI CRAB STICKS, HAND SHREDDED

4 CUPS COOKED RICE

1½ TBSP LIGHT SOY SAUCE

AS MUCH THINLY SLICED SPRING ONIONS AS YOU LIKE, TO GARNISH

1. Heat the vegetable oil in a wok and when hot, fry the onions until fragrant and light brown.

2. Add the chilli paste and stir until fragrant and the oil seeps out.

3. Break in the eggs and drizzle a little more oil over if the eggs start to stick.

4. Swirl the eggs around and scramble when half set.

5. Scatter the shredded crab sticks over and toss with the eggs.

6. Add the rice and soy sauce and stir well, turning the rice continuously until it is evenly coated with chilli.

7. Taste and add salt or a little more soy sauce if necessary, then add the spring onions and stir through.

8. Turn off the heat, dish out and serve immediately.

NASI LEMAK

MALAY COCONUT MILK AND PANDAN FLAVOURED RICE

Prep 5 mins | Cook 20 mins | Serves 2 – 3

Canned coconut milk is no longer difficult to come by and rice enriched by its addition goes well with so many dishes like chicken curry (page 47), achar (page 67), chicken wings (page 50), otah (page 33) and rendang (page 55).

300 G (2 LEVEL CUPS) JASMINE OR LONG GRAIN RICE, WASHED AND DRAINED IN A COLANDER OR LARGE SIEVE

300 ML (1½ CUPS) THICK COCONUT MILK

300 ML (1½ CUPS) WATER

2 TSP SALT

1 TSP SUGAR

6 FRESH OR FROZEN PANDAN LEAVES, WASHED AND KNOTTED

1. Combine all ingredients in a wide and heavy pot.

2. Stir well but gently to dissolve the salt and sugar.

3. Bring to a boil and cook until the liquid has almost evaporated and holes begin to appear on top of rice.

4. Cover the pot tightly and reduce heat to minimum.

5. Continue to cook for 10 minutes, then turn off the heat and leave covered and undisturbed for 15 minutes.

6. Open the pot, gently fluff the rice with fork and serve with the suggested dishes.

If fresh or frozen pandan leaves are unavailable, use ½ teaspoon pandan extract or 2 stalks trimmed and bashed fresh lemongrass.

EASY PEASY BRIYANI

SPICY CHICKEN AND GREEN PEA BASMATI PILAF

Prep 15 mins | Cook 25 mins | Serves 2 – 3

Sometimes you just want to give yourself a treat, and sometimes you're the designated cook for the dorm party, because let's face it, everyone needs to cut loose once in a while. But wait! You?! Cook for a party? Hell yes! This recipe will work whether you're cooking for two or 20. It's all up to you!

5 TBSP VEGETABLE OIL

1 LARGE ONION, PEELED, HALVED AND THINLY SLICED

2 TBSP PREPARED GINGER PASTE

1 TBSP PREPARED GARLIC PASTE

2 CHICKEN BREAST HALVES, CUT INTO LARGE CUBES

1 ROUNDED TBSP MEDIUM HOT CURRY POWDER

300 G (2 LEVEL CUPS) BASMATI RICE, WASHED AND DRAINED

600 ML (3 CUPS) LOW FAT CANNED CHICKEN STOCK OR BROTH

1½ TSP SALT

90 G (1 CUP) FROZEN BABY GREEN PEAS, THAWED AND DRAINED

1. Heat the oil in a heavy pot until hot but not smoking.

2. Fry the onion, ginger paste and garlic paste over medium heat until golden and fragrant.

3. Add the chicken and sprinkle over curry powder.

4. Stir until the chicken cubes brown.

5. Add the rice and stir gently until coated with oil.

6. Pour in the stock, add the salt and stir gently to dissolve the salt.

7. Bring to a boil, watch until the liquid is almost gone and holes begin to appear on top of rice.

8. Reduce heat to minimum, cover pot securely so the steam doesn't escape and cook for 10 minutes.

9. Open the pot, add peas, cover immediately and turn off the heat but do not open for 15 minutes.

10. Open the pot, gently fluff the rice with a fork and serve with achar (page 67).

Jasmine or Thai Hom Mali rice will do if you can't get basmati. One batch is 300 g (2 cups) raw rice. For every additional batch you cook, reduce the liquid and adjust the salt to taste, while maintaining the proportion of all other ingredients. For instance, 2 cups rice = 3 cups liquid, 4 cups rice = 5 cups liquid and 6 cups rice = 8 cups liquid. The amount of liquid needed per cup decreases as the amount of rice increases, though not necessarily by the same ratio.

Different rice brands or even different crops from the same brand absorb slightly different amounts of liquid. Practice will help you judge the amount needed.

If using a rice cooker, plug in the cooker and follow the recipe from steps 1 to 6, after which just put on the lid and ignore it until the switch changes from "Cook" mode to "Warm" mode. At this point, turn off the power but leave covered and undisturbed until ready to serve. Leaving the cooker in "Warm" mode will cause the bottom of the rice to burn.

Never promise to cook for a party, until you have assembled a wash and clean-up crew!

CHICKEN RICE

Prep 15 mins | Cook 30 mins | Serves 2–3

If you had to name just one dish that truly represents Singapore, chances are this is what would come to mind. I've tried to make this as uncomplicated as possible while retaining its essence and ability to transport you back home the fastest possible way, short of an air ticket. Enjoy!

1 TBSP SESAME OIL

2 TBSP LIGHT VEGETABLE OIL

2 TBSP PREPARED GINGER PASTE

1 TBSP PREPARED GARLIC PASTE

300 G (2 LEVEL CUPS) JASMINE OR LONG
    GRAIN RICE, WASHED AND DRAINED IN A
    COLANDER OR LARGE SIEVE

600 ML (3 CUPS) LOW FAT CANNED CHICKEN
    STOCK OR BROTH

1–2 TSP SALT

2 WHOLE CHICKEN LEGS, EACH CUT INTO 2
    AT THE JOINT

EXTRAS (OPTIONAL)

EXTRA SESAME OIL FOR DRESSING CHICKEN

LIGHT SOY SAUCE FOR DRESSING CHICKEN

AS MUCH CUCUMBER SLICES AS YOU LIKE

YOUR FAVOURITE PREPARED CHILLI, GINGER
    AND GARLIC SAUCE

> This dish also goes well with achar (page 67).

1. Combine the sesame and vegetable oil in a wide, deep pot and when moderately hot, fry the ginger and garlic paste until golden and fragrant.

2. Add the rice to the pot and stir until it is coated with oil.

3. Pour in the stock, add the salt and stir well, then bring to a boil. Immediately add the chicken pieces on top of the rice and continue to cook until almost all liquid has evaporated and small holes begin to appear on top of the rice.

4. Cover the pot tightly, turn heat down to an absolute minimum and leave it to cook for 20 minutes.

5. Open the cover and pierce the chicken at the thickest part, to the bone, with the tip of a small knife. There should be no blood and the juices should be clear.

6. Turn off the heat and cover the pot for 10 minutes. When ready to serve, remove the chicken to a plate.

7. Dish out the rice and top with your desired number of chicken pieces and cucumber slices.

8. Drizzle the chicken with sesame oil and soy sauce and serve with a side dish of chilli sauce.

LUNCHEON MEAT AND MUSHROOM RICE

Prep 15 mins | Cook 25 mins | Serves 2

Canned pork luncheon meat seems almost magical in its ability to comfort and restore when you're feeling homesick. We all know it's not the healthiest thing you can eat, but sometimes, "bad for you" is exactly what the soul seeks, especially on days when thoughts of home and family weigh heavily on the mind. Like the heart, the soul wants what the soul wants. Who are we to deny it?

4 TBSP VEGETABLE OIL

1 MEDIUM ONION, PEELED, HALVED AND SLICED

4 SLICES GINGER, PEELED

6 LARGE FRESH SHIITAKE MUSHROOMS, STEMMED AND THICKLY SLICED

1 CAN SPAM OR "MA LING" (IF YOU CAN FIND IT) PORK LUNCHEON MEAT, CUT INTO LARGE CUBES

300 G (2 LEVEL CUPS) JASMINE OR LONG GRAIN RICE, WASHED AND DRAINED IN A COLANDER OR LARGE SIEVE

600 ML (3 CUPS) LOW FAT CANNED CHICKEN STOCK OR BROTH

1 TSP SALT

1. Heat the vegetable oil in a heavy pot until hot but not smoking.

2. Fry the onion, ginger and mushrooms over medium heat until the onions are golden.

3. Add the luncheon meat and stir around now and then until the cubes start to brown.

4. Add the rice and stir until coated with oil.

5. Pour in the stock, add the salt and stir to dissolve the salt.

6. Bring to a boil, watch until the liquid is almost gone and holes begin to appear on top of the rice.

7. Reduce the heat to minimum, cover the pot securely and cook for 10 minutes.

8. Turn off the heat but leave the pot for another 15 minutes.

9. Open the pot, gently fluff the rice with a fork and serve in bowls.

For more flavour and crunch, drizzle the rice with some sesame oil and serve with your favourite chilli garlic sauce and slices of cucumber.

This also goes well with achar (page 67), in which case, omit the sesame oil and chilli sauce.

If using a rice cooker, follow recipe from steps 1 to 5, then cover the cooker and ignore it until it switches from "Cook" mode to "Warm" mode. Then turn off the cooker and leave undisturbed until ready to eat. Because this dish has oil in it, if left in "Warm" mode, the bottom of the rice will burn.

TEOCHEW MUAY
TEOCHEW STYLE PLAIN RICE PORRIDGE
Prep 3 mins | Cook 25 mins | Serves 2

In contrast to Cantonese congee, Teochew style rice porridge is grainy and almost soupy in consistency. Cooking it takes a mere 25 minutes.

75 G (½ CUP) UNCOOKED RICE, WASHED AND DRAINED
1 L (5 CUPS) WATER

1. Combine the rice and water in the deepest, narrowest pot (to reduce evaporation rate) you have and bring to a boil.

2. Turn the heat down to a very gentle simmer and put lid on. Make sure there is a slight gap between the pot and lid so that the mixture doesn't boil over and spill out.

3. Simmer for 20 minutes, stirring the porridge every few minutes, scraping the bottom of the pot so that the rice grains don't stick and burn.

4. Turn off the heat, cover the pot completely and leave undisturbed for 15−20 minutes to allow the rice grains to expand and tenderise further, without breaking down.

5. Serve the porridge with side dishes or garnishes as suggested for Cantonese Style Plain Rice Porridge (see next recipe).

CANTONESE STYLE PLAIN RICE PORRIDGE

Prep 3 mins | Cook 1½ hrs | Serves 2–3

Cantonese rice porridge is thick, with the grains so well cooked that they almost disappear into the broth. The long and gentle cooking breaks down the rice grains and imparts an incredibly smooth, almost velvety texture to the porridge. This is the kind of porridge you would probably want to eat when you're not feeling your best or when your stomach is not up to the task of digesting anything remotely robust.

**75 G (½ CUP) UNCOOKED RICE, WASHED
   AND DRAINED
1.6 L (8 CUPS) WATER**

Serve with cooked or side dishes of your choice like crispy fried salted anchovies, prawn omelette (page 31), stir-fried Asian greens (page 68) or pork balls with napa cabbage (page 46).

Alternatively, garnish the porridge with crisp shallots, sliced red chillies, sliced spring onions, a drizzle of sesame oil and light soy sauce to taste, for a very simple and light meal.

To cook in a slow cooker, reduce the water to 4 cups, put the ingredients in, put the lid on (leaving a slight gap to prevent over boiling) and set on "Low". When mixture starts to bubble and thicken, stir occasionally to prevent sticking. When the porridge has reached the desired consistency, turn off the heat and serve as suggested.

1. Combine the rice and water in the deepest, narrowest pot (to reduce evaporation rate) you have and bring to a boil.

2. Turn the heat down to a very gentle simmer and put lid on. Make sure there is a slight gap between the pot and lid so mixture doesn't boil over and spill out.

3. Stir the porridge every 10–15 minutes, scraping the bottom of the pot so that the rice grains don't stick and burn.

4. As the rice grains expand and start to break down (after 45 minutes or so), stir the porridge more often as it will tend to stick even more.

5. When the rice grains have broken down and the porridge is thick and smooth, turn off the heat. If you find the porridge too thick, dilute slightly with hot water.

WHITE RICE

Prep 5 mins | Cook 20 mins | Serves 2 (or 3 small eaters)

No self respecting son or daughter of Singapore should leave home without knowing how to cook this. It has myriad applications from fried rice, to char siew fan, to congee. When my then 18-year-old husband didn't have his mum on call 24/7, he survived on white rice and Kentucky Fried Chicken. When he got bored with fried chicken, he got by on white rice and sliced kiwifruit. I don't want things to be so dire for you, hence this cookbook. If you've watched *Survivor* you will know that even professional chefs can screw this up. Pay attention.

300 G (2 LEVEL CUPS) UNCOOKED LONG
   GRAIN RICE (UNBROKEN THAI HOM MALI
   OR JASMINE RICE IS WHAT YOUR MUM
   PROBABLY COOKS AT HOME, BASMATI RICE
   IS GOOD WITH INDIAN FOOD)
600 ML (3 CUPS) WATER

1. Wash the rice gently in 2 or 3 changes of water or until the water is almost clear. Don't manhandle the rice, the grains are quite delicate when wet and break easily.

2. Drain the rice in a colander or sieve if you have one. If not, try your best to pour out all the water without spilling the rice into the sink. To do so, use your palm with fingers pressed tightly together as a barrier to stop the rice from following the water that's being poured out.

3. Pour the measured out clean water into the pot with the washed rice.

4. Put the pot to boil and allow almost all the water to evaporate until you can see little holes appearing on top of the rice.

5. Cover the pot tightly and bring heat down to minimum. The smaller the flame or the lower the heat, the better.

6. Leave to cook for 10 minutes, then turn off heat.

7. Leave the pot covered and undisturbed for 15 minutes, then open the lid and gently fluff up the rice with a fork.

WATER AND RICE MEASUREMENTS

1 cup rice	$1\frac{1}{2}$ cups water
2 cups rice	3 cups water
3 cups rice	4 cups water
4 cups rice	5 cups water
5 cups rice	6 cups water
6 cups rice	$7\frac{1}{2}$ cups water
7 cups rice	9 cups water
8 cups rice	10 cups water

Use the same cup to measure out both the rice and water or the rice may not turn out as desired.

SWEET TREATS

ALMOND JELLY WITH LONGAN

BLACK AND WHITE NO-BAKE CHEESECAKE

BUBUR CHA CHA

GORENG PISANG

BUBUR MANIS

CHOCOLATE AND COCONUT BABY CAKES

BREAD PUDDING

JAM ROLLS

CHOCOLATE CHIP MUG CAKE

BROWN SUGAR AND COCONUT AGAR-AGAR

DOUBLE PEANUT COOKIES

SWEET RED BEAN SOUP

MUA CHEE

SUGAR CANE AND LIME JELLIES

NO PASTRY FRUIT PIE

POLKA DOT SLICES

TANG YUAN

SWEET POTATO IN GINGER SYRUP

COCONUT CANDY

ALMOND JELLY WITH LONGAN

Prep 5 mins | Cook 15 mins | Serves 3 – 4

When I was a child, I hated almond jelly, but strangely enough, when my boys developed a liking for it from constant exposure at class parties in school, I got sucked in along with them. Now I find it irresistible combined with longans or other tropical fruit in syrup. A bowl of thoroughly chilled cubes or scoops of almond jelly amid a tumble of crisp, cold and juicy fruit is a godsend during the hottest months of the year!

2½–3 TSP AGAR-AGAR POWDER (DEPENDING
   ON HOW FIRM YOU LIKE IT)
800 ML (4 CUPS) WATER
100 ML (½ CUP) EVAPORATED MILK
75 G (½ CUP) SUGAR
½–1 TSP ALMOND ESSENCE OR
   ALMOND EXTRACT
1 LARGE CAN LONGANS IN SYRUP,
   WELL CHILLED

1. Combine the agar-agar powder, water, milk and sugar in a pot or pan and bring to a boil over medium heat.

2. Stir until the sugar dissolves, taking care not to let liquid boil over.

3. Turn off the heat and stir in the almond essence or extract. Allow the mixture to cool slightly, then pour through a strainer into a shallow baking tray or dish.

4. Leave at room temperature until cool before chilling until completely set and very cold.

5. To serve, cut the jelly into small cubes or scoop up the pieces with a spoon. Put the desired amount into individual bowls, cups or glasses and top with your desired amount of cold longans and syrup.

You don't have to strain the liquid into the tray if no "skin" has formed on the surface upon cooling. This tends to happen because of the milk and if you leave the mixture to sit for too long. If there is no "skin", just pour the mixture into the tray.

While I like this best with longans, you can also serve it with pineapple cubes, lychees, melon balls or cubes, seeded rambutans, and so on.

A drained maraschino cherry with stem and a small sprig of mint make a very simple but pretty garnish that will elevate this very simple dessert to something you can proudly serve guests for a lovely finish to a special meal.

BLACK AND WHITE NO-BAKE CHEESECAKE

Prep 20 mins | Chill 6 hrs | Serves 4

(but I'd understand if you don't want to share this)

Cheesecake is my dessert weakness and if you're like at least half of the human race, you probably get weak at the knees at the sight of it too. The dark chocolate cookie crust contrasts beautifully with the tangy cheese filling, but if you find the filling sour, increase the sugar by the tablespoon as you mix, until it tastes right to you. Cheesecake is easy, but cheesecake is not cheap because cheese is not cheap. Stop being easy prey and learn to make your own. Never buy another cheesecake again!

30 PIECES DARK CHOCOLATE SANDWICH COOKIES (LIKE OREO)

250 G (1 CARTON OR BRICK) SOFT CREAM CHEESE (PHILADELPHIA CHEESE WORKS VERY WELL)

100 G (⅔ CUP) CASTOR SUGAR

200 G (1 CARTON OR 1 CUP) SOUR CREAM

5 TSP LEMON JELLY CRYSTALS

2 TSP VANILLA EXTRACT

120 G (1 CUP) READY WHIPPED CREAM OR NON-DAIRY WHIPPED TOPPING (LIKE COOL WHIP)

1. Line a 20 cm round cake tin or deep pie dish with cling wrap, making sure there is a generous overhang.

2. Arrange the cookies in a dish or tin to cover the base as best as you can, breaking some cookies into quarters to patch up awkward spaces.

3. Slightly wet one side of some cookies and "stick" the wet side to the inner side of the tin or dish.

4. In a large mixing bowl, combine the cheese, sugar, sour cream, jelly crystals and vanilla extract and stir thoroughly but gently with a whisk until smooth, but do not beat the mixture.

5. Very gently stir in the whipped cream or non-dairy whipped topping until well combined.

6. Gently pour and scrape the cheese mixture into the cookie lined tin or dish and gently smooth the top.

7. Chill for 6 hours or until it sets.

8. Using the plastic overhang, gently ease out and pull out the cheesecake from the tin and transfer to the plate.

9. Cut off the plastic as best you can without damaging the cake. Cut and serve. Store leftovers covered in the fridge and eat within 3 days.

BUBUR CHA CHA

SWEET POTATO AND YAM PORRIDGE

Prep 20 mins | Cook 25 mins | Serves 2–4

I've been asked repeatedly what bubur cha cha means but I remain as foggy as the origin of this delightful dessert's name. It is either a Chinese Peranakan or Malay creation, and its name could mean "mixed porridge" or it could be a completely random name given by its creator who was in a mischievous mood when asked "What's for dessert?" I suspect though, that the genius behind this culinary gem was a whimsical soul with a gift for improvisation, who liked the word "cha" so much, she said it twice!

3 SMALL SWEET POTATOES (ABOUT 300 G),
   PEELED AND SOAKED IN WATER TO
   PREVENT DARKENING
½ MEDIUM-SIZED YAM (ABOUT 300 G),
   THICKLY PEELED
30 G (⅓ CUP) MEDIUM GRAIN PEARL SAGO
400 ML (2 CUPS) WATER
400 ML (2 CUPS) THICK COCONUT MILK
200 G (1⅓ CUPS) SUGAR
4 FRESH OR FROZEN PANDAN LEAVES, WASHED
   AND KNOTTED (OR 1 TSP PANDAN ESSENCE
   OR EXTRACT)
A GENEROUS PINCH OF SALT

If you find the preparation too involved, you could omit the pearl sago and save yourself some additional cooking and pot washing. The dessert will still be delicious but I have to tell you that I find the tiny, starchy and slightly chewy spheres delightful to bite into.

1. Cut the sweet potatoes and yam into small (1 cm) pieces and steam over rapidly boiling water for about 15 minutes or until the cubes are easily pierced with a toothpick but retain their shape. Remove from the steamer and set aside.

2. Put a small pot of water to boil while the sweet potatoes and yam steam. When boiling, pour in the pearl sago and cook until translucent, stirring often to prevent sticking.

3. Pour the cooked sago through a fine sieve to drain, and rinse under cold tap water until the water runs clear. Soak the sago in a bowl of really cold water to prevent sticking.

4. Combine the water, coconut milk, sugar, pandan and salt in a pot and bring to a boil. Stir to dissolve the sugar.

5. When the mixture boils, lower the heat immediately and keep stirring to prevent the coconut milk from separating.

6. Add in the sweet potatoes, yam and well drained sago, and stir well to combine and heat through. Turn off the heat and cool slightly. Discard the pandan and serve hot or cold.

GORENG PISANG

BATTERED FRIED BANANAS

Prep 10 mins | Cook 15 mins | Makes 8 pieces

Bananas make a delicious snack as they are, but when dipped in batter and fried to a golden crisp, they really come into their own. No other fruit I can think of turns so utterly and decadently delicious when cooked. Debates rage on about whether goreng pisang or pisang goreng is correct. If you're curious, pisang goreng means "fried bananas" and goreng pisang means "fry bananas". In Singapore, while ungrammatical, "goreng pisang" is the de facto term. Debate feeds the mind, but not the stomach, so start slicing those bananas and heat that pan!

300 ML (1½ CUPS OR ENOUGH TO ACHIEVE A
   DEPTH OF 4 CM IN THE PAN) VEGETABLE OIL
75 G (¾ CUP) PLAIN OR ALL-PURPOSE FLOUR
75 G (¾ CUP) RICE FLOUR
½ TSP BAKING POWDER
½ TSP SALT
150 ML (¾ CUP) WATER
4 LARGE RIPE BANANAS, PEELED AND
   HALVED LENGTHWISE

1. Slowly heat the oil in a deep pan until moderately hot.

2. While the oil heats, combine all the dry ingredients in a large mixing bowl and whisk together.

3. Pour in the water and stir lightly with whisk until you get a thick (enough to easily coat a spoon) and smooth batter. **Do not overmix**.

4. Turn up the heat to medium and dip the banana halves in batter to completely and thickly coat.

5. Gently lower the bananas in hot oil and cook until golden and crisp, turning over a few times, to ensure even cooking.

6. Remove from the pan and drain on crushed kitchen paper. Repeat with the remaining banana halves.

7. Serve while still hot.

To achieve the crackly and feathered appearance and texture of hawker style goreng pisang, dilute a bit of batter to an easy pouring consistency and drizzle this with your fingers, back and forth over the banana halves as they fry in the pan.

The traditional banana for goreng pisang is pisang raja, also known as musa belle. It would be great if you can find this variety, but the easily available Cavendish banana will do fine.

Leftover goreng pisang should be stored and reheated as for curry puffs (page 14).

BUBUR MANIS
SWEET MALAY STYLE FRAGRANT PORRIDGE
Prep 5 mins | Cook 10 mins | Serves 2

Bubur terigu or sweet wheatberry porridge is a local favourite amongst those who prefer an Asian flavour to their desserts. It is deliciously chewy with a lovely nutty, almost creamy flavour but it takes hours of gentle simmering to crack those hardy wheat kernels and bring out their best. Here's something much quicker, just as delicious and possibly more nutritious. If you love oats, you may never want to eat it any other way again.

100 G (1 CUP) MEDIUM OATS
400 ML (2 CUPS) WATER
60 G (½ CUP) SOFT BROWN SUGAR
3 FRESH OR FROZEN PANDAN LEAVES, WASHED AND KNOTTED
A GENEROUS PINCH OF SALT
100 ML (½ CUP) THICK COCONUT MILK

1. Combine all the ingredients in a pot, except for the coconut milk.

2. Stir well to dissolve the sugar and bring to a boil.

3. Reduce the heat and simmer for about 5 minutes or until the oats are as tender as you like.

4. Pour in the coconut milk and heat through, while stirring.

5. Turn off the heat as soon as it comes to a boil again.

6. Discard the pandan leaves and serve in bowls.

If pandan leaves are not available fresh or frozen, do not use dried leaves. Instead, substitute with 1 teaspoon of vanilla extract or ½ teaspoon of pandan essence.

CHOCOLATE AND COCONUT BABY CAKES

Prep 15 mins | Cook 20 mins | Makes 10

You could grab a box of instant mix and stir up a cake in a jiffy, and, while I don't mind canned food, instant stock and many other instant foods, cake mixes are not my thing as even with lots of kitchen intervention, they have this pronounced and difficult to disguise chemical aftertaste that just spoils it for me. These super moist bites of chocolate and coconut heaven are just a very lazy stir away. No more excuses!

70 ML (⅓ CUP) LIGHT VEGETABLE OIL (SOY OR CANOLA IS BEST)
100 G (1⅔ CUP) DESICCATED (DRIED GRATED) COCONUT
120 G (¾ CUP) CASTOR SUGAR
75 G (¾ CUP) PLAIN FLOUR
1 TSP BAKING SODA (SIFTED INTO THE PLAIN FLOUR)
4 TBSP PLAIN UNSWEETENED YOGHURT OR SOUR CREAM
1 TSP VANILLA EXTRACT
100 G (¾ CUP) MINI DARK CHOCOLATE CHIPS

1. Preheat the oven at 180°C and line a muffin tin with 10 paper muffin cases.

2. Combine all the ingredients in a large mixing bowl and stir to mix everything until smooth. **Do not over mix.**

3. Divide the mixture evenly between muffin cases (an ice cream scoop is best for this).

4. Bake for 20 minutes or until golden on top.

5. Test the centre of a few of the cakes with a skewer, toothpick or thin, pointy knife. The tip should come out free of batter.

6. When done, remove from the oven and take the cakes out of tin when they have cooled slightly. Serve warm or cold with coffee, tea or milk.

BREAD PUDDING

Prep 15 mins | Cook 50 mins | Serves 4

Though it's said to have originated from England, many cultures are familiar with some kind of bread pudding. In Singapore and Malaysia, there is even a version called bingka roti which uses coconut milk instead of dairy milk. I'm giving you the recipe that my grandmother and mother always used (if you can call a cup of this, a spoon of that and two pinches of another, a recipe). Both women were products of the "waste not want not" era, so the recipe is frugal. There are no bells or whistles, just tender and moist pudding, so fragrant, I'm sure the angels in heaven can smell it baking.

300 G STALE (BUT NOT MOULDY!) BREAD
   (10 SLICES SANDWICH BREAD OR A
   SMALL BAGUETTE)
400 ML (2 CUPS) MILK
50 G (⅓ CUP) BUTTER
100 G (⅔ CUP) SUGAR
3 LARGE EGGS
1½ TSP GROUND CINNAMON
½ TSP GROUND NUTMEG
2 TSP VANILLA EXTRACT
2 TBSP EXTRA SUGAR (DEMERARA SUGAR
   IS LOVELY BUT REGULAR WILL DO), FOR
   SCATTERING OVER PUDDING

This is magnificent served warm and crusty, with a scoop of rich and not too sweet (okay, I mean expensive) vanilla ice cream. It's always fun (and oh-so-delicious) when rich slums with poor. ;)

1. Preheat the oven at 180°C and generously butter a 23 cm square or 30 cm by 20 cm rectangular baking tin or dish.

2. Cut the bread into cubes (about 1 cm) and scatter in an even layer in the buttered dish.

3. Combine the milk, butter and sugar in a small pot and heat gently, stirring until the butter and sugar melt. Turn off the heat immediately and allow to cool.

4. In a separate large bowl, whisk together the eggs, spices and vanilla until the egg whites are no longer visible. Pour the cooled (or warm, but not hot) milk mixture over the eggs and whisk together until thoroughly combined.

5. Pour the milk and egg mixture evenly over the bread in the dish. Push the bread into the mixture until every bit is soaked in the liquid.

6. Leave to soak for at least 20 minutes, better yet until the bread has absorbed the liquid and swelled up.

7. Scatter the extra sugar over the pudding and bake for 50 minutes or until the top is golden and crusty. Remove from the oven and cool for 20 minutes before serving in thick slices.

JAM ROLLS

Prep 15 mins | Cook 15 mins | Makes 12 rolls

When you're feeling hungry or just peckish in the afternoon, but dinner is still some way off, I doubt an apple will do the trick, if you're anything like me. There are times when only a sugar hit will do and these are really quick, really easy and so good with a cup of hot tea. Be sure to get really good jam with lots of fruit chunks in it. If you don't like jam, orange or lemon curd, chocolate spread or kaya, if you can find it, are all as lovely.

300 G (3 LEVEL CUPS) PLAIN FLOUR

3 TSP BAKING POWDER

2 TBSP CASTOR SUGAR

80 G (½ CUP) VERY SOFT BUTTER

175 ML (SLIGHTLY OVER ¾ CUP) BUTTERMILK
**   OR REGULAR MILK**

100 G (½ CUP) CHUNKY JAM (I LIKE STRAWBERRY
**   OR RASPBERRY JAM)**

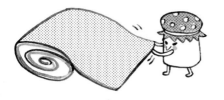

1. Preheat the oven at 190°C and line a baking tray with baking parchment.

2. Combine the flour, baking powder and sugar in a large mixing bowl and stir with a whisk.

3. Add the butter and stir very quickly and lightly with a blunt knife until it is rough and crumbly.

4. Pour in the milk all at once and stir until a soft dough starts to form. Stop stirring immediately.

5. Push the mixture together with your hands until you have a smooth dough, but do not knead. Turn out onto a clean surface very lightly dusted with flour.

6. Pat into an even rectangle about 30 cm by 20 cm and spread with jam or other filling.

7. Starting from the longer edge closest to you, roll up like a carpet and pinch the seam to seal.

8. Take a sharp knife and gently slice across into 12 even pieces.

9. Lay the pieces on a tray and bake for 15 minutes or until golden and risen.

10. Remove from the oven and transfer the rolls to a cooling rack before serving.

CHOCOLATE CHIP MUG CAKE

Prep 10 mins | *Cook 2 mins* | *Serves 1 rabid chocoholic (barely)*

You're probably thinking this hasn't got much going for it, apart from shock value or weird science novelty. Hah! Try it and you'll see. Nuking food is always fun, but eater beware, this stuff is dangerous. Imagine being able to have sinfully good chocolate cake any time you want, in the absence of a 24/7 convenience store, night or day, at the touch of a button. *gasp* You now hold the sticky, chocolate smeared key to the kingdom; use it wisely, or prepare to invest in a pair of stretchy fat pants. You have been warned.

4 TBSP SELF-RAISING FLOUR (OR 4 TBSP PLAIN
    FLOUR PLUS 1 TSP BAKING POWDER)
4 TBSP SOFT BROWN SUGAR OR WHITE SUGAR
2 TBSP PURE UNSWEETENED COCOA POWDER
4 TBSP MINI CHOCOLATE CHIPS
1 EGG
3 TBSP MILK
3 TBSP VEGETABLE OIL
1–2 TSP VANILLA EXTRACT

1. Combine the flour, sugar, cocoa and chocolate chips in the biggest coffee mug you have and stir thoroughly.

3. Break in the egg and add the milk, oil and vanilla extract.

4. Stir until well mixed and scrape the mixture down sides of the mug.

5. Cook mixture in microwave for 1 minute on "Medium". The mixture will puff up.

6. Allow it to sink back into mug, then cook again for 30 seconds on "Medium".

7. Remove from the microwave and let it stand on the counter until it cools enough to eat without burning your mouth.

Chocolate is good, but try eating an apple once in a while.
    Failing that, show all your dorm mates and friends how to do this, so stretchy pants become trendy.

BROWN SUGAR AND COCONUT AGAR-AGAR
BROWN SUGAR AND COCONUT JELLY

Prep 10 mins | Cook 5 mins | Serves 3–4

So simple, yet so delicious and hardly made or eaten as often as it should be. Traditionally, palm sugar (gula melaka) is used for that unmistakably rich and caramel-like tropical flavour, but I don't think you will easily find it in the west. Soft, moist dark brown sugar makes a very decent substitute. Of course if you are lucky enough to find it, scrape off an equivalent amount from a block. It's bothersome, but if you have tasted soft, gooey palm sugar, you will know it's delicious enough to nibble on as it is and will lend the same irresistible flavour to everything it touches.

2½–3 TSP AGAR-AGAR POWDER (DEPENDING ON HOW FIRM YOU LIKE IT)
700 ML (3½ CUPS) WATER
80 G (⅔ CUP) SOFT DARK BROWN SUGAR
4 FRESH OR FROZEN PANDAN LEAVES, WASHED AND KNOTTED (OR 1 TSP PANDAN ESSENCE OR EXTRACT)
⅓ TSP SALT
200 ML (1 CUP) THICK COCONUT MILK

1. Combine the agar-agar powder, water, sugar, pandan leaves and salt in a pot or pan and bring to a boil over moderate heat.

2. Stir until the sugar dissolves, taking care not to let the liquid boil over. Stir in the coconut milk and bring it back to a boil.

3. Turn off the heat and stir to prevent the coconut milk from curdling. Allow the mixture to cool slightly, then pour through a strainer into a shallow baking tray or dish. Discard the pandan leaves.

4. Leave the mixture at room temperature until cool or at least warm before chilling until it is completely set and very cold. Slice into squares, diamonds or rectangles and serve.

Don't skip the straining step as dark brown sugar and especially palm sugar tend to contain tiny impurities like grit or fibrous flecks.

If using pandan essence or extract, add it after turning off the heat to retain as much of the fragrance as possible, as boiling will cause some of the fragrance to dissipate.

If you are bored with the usual square or diamond shapes, jazz up presentation by cutting out the agar-agar with large, unusually shaped cookie cutters. Don't use anything too intricate as the delicate bits will tend to break off. There will be more "wastage" but you could always gather up the odd bits and serve over ice cream or in a glass of iced tea or your favourite cold beverage.

DOUBLE PEANUT COOKIES

Prep 5 mins | Cook 15 mins | Makes 18

These are probably the easiest, and if you're a peanut butter lover, the yummiest cookies you will ever make and eat. Child's play, I kid you not!

150 G (1 CUP) SMOOTH PEANUT BUTTER
75 G (½ CUP) CASTOR SUGAR
1 EGG
60 G (½ CUP) CHOPPED PEANUTS (ALMONDS ARE NICE TOO)
1 TSP VANILLA EXTRACT

If you don't want to chill cookie mix before baking, instead of forming balls, drop spoonfuls equally apart on the baking tray and bake according to recipe. Chilling will firm the dough up, make it less sticky for easier handling and will produce rounder, higher, more uniform shaped cookies. If you don't mind rough and uneven shaped cookies, you can skip this step.

For a real treat, roughly crumble cookies over scoops of vanilla ice cream and drizzle everything generously with chocolate syrup or fudge topping.

1. Combine all ingredients in a large mixing bowl and stir until well mixed.

2. Cover and chill mixture for 30 minutes.

3. Preheat oven at 165°C and line a baking sheet or tray with baking parchment.

4. Take out the mixture and divide into 18 balls.

5. Put the balls on a tray, space equally apart and flatten each ball with a fork.

6. Bake for 12−15 minutes or until golden.

7. Remove from the oven and cool the cookies for 5 minutes before transferring them to a cooling rack.

SWEET RED BEAN SOUP

Prep 8 hrs (including soaking) | Cook 1 hr 30 mins | Serves 4

Ooh! Big bad beans!! We all know about the bean's nasty reputation where gastrointestinal discomfort and other less than desirable effects (mostly of the sound variety) are concerned. But a citrus scented sweet broth of tender, slow simmered red beans is worth every agony and embarrassment. No, I'm just kidding— have your soup, with your glamour intact. All it takes is a long soak in a warm baking soda bath; for the beans, not for you.

200 G (1⅓ CUPS) RED BEANS OR ADZUKI BEANS

½ TSP BAKING SODA

1.2 L (6 CUPS) WATER

2 LARGE STRIPS DRIED TANGERINE PEEL

1 CAN COOKED LOTUS SEEDS, DRAINED (OPTIONAL)

100 G (⅔ CUP) SUGAR

1. Wash and drain the red beans and put into a large bowl or container. Cover the beans with warm water and stir in the baking soda. Leave to soak for 4–8 hours.

2. Drain off the soaking water, rinse the beans and drain again. Put beans into a pot and add the 1.2 L of water and tangerine peels.

3. Bring to a boil and simmer, partially covered, until the beans are tender but not mushy. If the mixture gets too thick, add more water to achieve desired consistency.

4. Add the drained lotus seeds and stir. They should be already tender straight out of the can but if not, cook until they are as soft as you like.

5. Gently stir in the sugar until it's dissolved and turn off heat. Discard the tangerine peel and serve.

The addition of tangerine peel and lotus seeds are traditional but they are a bit of an acquired taste. If unavailable or simply not to your taste, just omit them. You could instead flavour the broth with fresh or frozen pandan leaves or slices of peeled fresh ginger, or both, if you prefer. Just add them to the pot together with the beans and water.

If you cannot find pandan in any form, 1 teaspoon of pandan essence or extract added together with the sugar, will make an acceptable substitute.

There is some debate as to whether or not soaking beans with baking soda reduces flatulence. Personally I find it works for me. It is true however, that baking soda tenderises the skin on beans and makes them break down more quickly, which may indirectly render them more digestable and less likely to cause trouble in the gut. Omit this step, if you wish, but the beans will take longer to cook.

MUA CHEE

GLUTINOUS RICE DOUGH IN PEANUT AND SESAME COATING

Prep 10 mins | Cook 5 mins | Serves 2–4

I would not be surprised if you've never tasted mua chee, as it is nowhere near as common as it used to be in Singapore. Said to be of Southern Chinese origin, mua chee means sesame cake in Hokkien. In Cantonese it is called loh mai chee and means dough cake. It doesn't seem farfetched actually, to even compare it to the Japanese mochi, but enough speculation. Mua chee can be found in Malaysia, Hong Kong and Taiwan as well and it's easy to understand its widespread popularity; cheap ingredients and simple preparation adding up to an addictively delicious treat.

100 G (1 LEVEL CUP) GLUTINOUS RICE FLOUR

1 TBSP TAPIOCA FLOUR

½ TSP SALT

4 TBSP THICK COCONUT MILK

150 ML (¾ CUP) WATER

2 TBSP ONION OIL (LEFTOVER OIL FROM
    FRYING SHALLOT CRISP)

60 G (½ CUP) TOASTED PEANUTS, CHOPPED
    FINE (I PULSE THEM IN A COFFEE GRINDER)

A GENEROUS TBSP TOASTED SESAME SEEDS

50 G (⅓ CUP) CASTOR SUGAR

1. Combine the glutinous rice flour, tapioca flour, salt, coconut milk and water in a mixing bowl and stir until well mixed. Thoroughly grease a tray with the onion oil.

2. Pour the mixture into the tray and steam over high heat for about 20 minutes or until cooked and quite firm, right through.

3. Remove from the steamer and allow to cool.

4. Combine the peanuts, sesame seeds and sugar in a large plate and set aside.

5. To serve, use a pair of oiled scissors to snip off a strip of the dough from the tray (enough for one person) and place on the peanut mixture. Snip the strip into small, bite size pieces, tossing pieces around in the peanut mix until thoroughly coated.

6. Transfer the coated dough pieces to a saucer and serve with toothpicks. Repeat with the rest of the dough and coating for each required serving.

If you don't have onion oil, just use ordinary vegetable oil with 2 or 3 drops of sesame oil, for fragrance.

The coconut milk is not traditional, but makes the dough richer, tender and even more delicious.

SUGAR CANE AND LIME JELLIES

Prep 10 mins | Cook 2 mins | Makes 4 jellies

Sugar cane and lime juice is a fantastic way to cool off when tropical temperatures soar in the middle of the year. While temperatures in most other locations are relatively cooler, summers can still really sizzle! When the heat gets too much, cool down with these simple but delightfully refreshing jellies. Canned tropical juices are now quite readily available in most supermarkets worldwide. Take a look around, you might be surprised by what you find.

1 CAN SUGAR CANE JUICE
**JUICE OF HALF A LIME (IF YOU PREFER A
    STRONGER LIME FLAVOUR)**
200 ML (1 CUP) WATER
1 PACKET SWEETENED LIME JELLY CRYSTALS

1. Combine the sugar cane juice, lime juice and water in a pot and heat until very hot but not boiling.

2. Stir in the jelly crystals until completely dissolved.

3. Divide the jelly mixture amongst 4 small cups or jelly moulds and leave on the counter to cool until warm.

4. Take a toothpick and burst any bubbles on the jelly mixture surface and chill in fridge until completely set.

5. Dip the jelly moulds half deep in very hot water for a few seconds, then turn jellies out onto a saucer to serve. Or, just eat straight out of the mould.

Garnish each saucer with slices of your favourite fresh tropical fruit for a healthier and visually appealing dessert.

Replace sugar cane juice with coconut, guava or soursop juice. For soursop juice, you may prefer to omit the lime juice as soursop (known as guanabana in some countries) is quite tangy on its own.

NO PASTRY FRUIT PIE

Prep 15 mins | Cook 50 mins | Serves 4

Pastry isn't difficult to make, still, many view it with suspicion or even anxiety. But, just because you don't want to mess around with it or even just thaw and roll out the commercial stuff doesn't mean you can't have your pie and bloody well eat it too. This luscious but fabulously easy and fuss free pie will likely become a permanent fixture in your kitchen repertoire, even if you are an old hand at pastry making.

1 CAN (ABOUT 450 G) FRUIT PIE FILLING
   (CHERRY IS MY FAVOURITE, CLOSELY
   FOLLOWED BY APPLE)
1 TSP GROUND CINNAMON
150 G (1 CUP) CASTOR SUGAR
150 G (1 PACKED CUP) BUTTER, MELTED
60 G (½ CUP) CHOPPED NUTS (I LIKE PECANS
   OR ALMONDS)
1 EGG
1–2 TSP VANILLA EXTRACT
⅓ TSP FINE SALT
150 G (1½ CUPS) PLAIN FLOUR

1. Preheat the oven at 180°C and generously brush a 23 cm pie dish with some of the melted butter.

2. Pour the pie filling into a pie dish, sprinkle over the cinnamon and stir lightly to mix.

3. Mix the sugar, butter, nuts, egg, vanilla and salt in a separate large mixing bowl and stir to dissolve sugar.

4. Add the flour and stir in lightly until there are no lumps.

5. Spread this mixture evenly over the fruit in the pie dish until the fruit is completely and neatly covered.

6. Bake for 50 minutes or until golden and crisp on top.

7. Remove from the oven and cool before cutting.

> For a really indulgent dessert, serve with a scoop of vanilla ice cream on the side and drizzle over readymade butterscotch or caramel sauce.

POLKA DOT SLICES

Prep 10 mins | Cook 20 mins | Makes 16 slices

That box of pancake mix I convinced you to buy has more uses than you may realise. Got milk? Got chocolate chips? Then you got dessert! These are not too sweet, but the abundance of chocolate chips definitely makes up for it. They're good as they are, but if you can go the extra mile, the simple icing does give them a little more dessert cred.

200 G (2 CUPS) INSTANT PANCAKE MIX
  (I RECOMMEND BETTY CROCKER BRAND)
50 G (⅓ CUP) CASTOR SUGAR
300 ML (1½ CUPS) MILK
2 TSP VANILLA EXTRACT
150 G (1¼ CUPS) MINI DARK CHOCOLATE CHIPS

ICING (OPTIONAL)
100 G (1 CUP) ICING OR CONFECTIONER'S SUGAR
3 TBSP WATER OR LEMON JUICE IF YOU PREFER
  THIS NOT TOO SWEET

1. Preheat the oven at 180°C and line a baking tray with baking parchment.

2. In a large mixing bowl, combine the pancake mix, sugar, milk, vanilla extract and half of chocolate chips.

3. Stir with a whisk to combine everything. **Do not over mix**.

4. Scrape the batter into a baking tray and scatter the top evenly with the remaining chocolate chips.

5. Bake for 20 minutes or until risen and pale gold.

6. Remove from the oven and leave until completely cold.

7. To make the icing, combine the ingredients and stir with a whisk until very smooth. It should be thick but pourable.

8. Pour the icing evenly over cake and spread with a spatula to completely cover the cake.

9. Leave to set (at least 30 minutes—faster under a fan or by a breezy window) before cutting into rectangles.

TANG YUAN
GLUTINOUS RICE BALLS IN FRAGRANT SYRUP
Prep 15 mins (excluding chilling) | Cook 10 mins | Serves 4

You would think that a simple bowl of rice flour balls in syrup holds hardly any draw, but bite into one, bathed in a fragrant, sweet syrup and you may just find your socks charmed off by this unassuming dessert. Its simple looks belie the fact that this is a dessert rich with symbolism for the Chinese—it is traditionally eaten on the first day of winter and is also often served on auspicious occasions like birthdays and anniversaries to signify reunions and the passing of another year. The little spheres also represent wholeness and togetherness in a family. Who would have thought?

200 G (2 CUPS) GLUTINOUS RICE FLOUR
150 ML (¾ CUP) WATER
75 G (½ CUP) SUGAR
1–2 DROPS FOOD COLOURING (ANY COLOURS
    YOU LIKE)
400 ML (2 CUPS) WATER
4 FRESH OR FROZEN PANDAN LEAVES, WASHED
    AND KNOTTED
2 SLICES GINGER, PEELED (OPTIONAL)

1. Combine the flour, water and 2 tablespoons sugar in a large mixing bowl and mix with your hands until a dough forms.

2. Knead the dough until no longer sticky and divide into 2–4 portions.

3. Add a few drops of different food colours to each portion of dough and knead in until the colour is evenly distributed. Just a few drops will do or the finished colours will be garish.

4. Form the dough portions into small balls, rolling them between your palms until smooth and without cracks. Put balls on a plate or tray in a layer, cover lightly and chill for 2–4 hours. This prevents cracks and helps them retain their shape when cooking.

5. Prepare the syrup by combining the remaining sugar, water, pandan and ginger in a small pot and bring to a boil. Stir until the sugar is dissolved and simmer for about 10 minutes to extract flavour from the pandan and ginger. Discard the ginger and pandan.

6. Bring another small pot of water to a boil. When boiling, drop in the balls (not too many at once or they might stick) and cook gently until they float to the surface.

7. Remove from the pot and add to the syrup. Repeat with the remaining balls.

8. Dish out the balls with the syrup and serve. You may cool down the dessert and chill before serving.

The cooked and cooled balls may be served with ice cream and go especially well with green tea ice cream and cooked, sweetened red beans, like mochi balls would. They also add a delicious bite and texture to red bean soup (page 115), bubur cha cha (page 106), sweet potato in ginger syrup (page 122) or your favourite sweet Asian dessert porridge or soup like bubur pulut hitam, bubur terigu or cheng teng.

Try very small balls in iced tea, green tea or cold sweetened soy milk for a different take on the popular Taiwanese pearl tea.

If you don't mind the effort and a bit of a mess, try stuffing the dough with balls of prepared red bean paste, frozen balls of peanut butter, sweetened sesame paste or canned pumpkin paste before shaping, chilling and cooking. Don't overstuff balls and make sure the filling is completely sealed to prevent the dough from cracking and the filling from leaking out.

SWEET POTATO IN GINGER SYRUP

Prep 10 mins | Cook 40 mins | Serves 2–4

Sweet potatoes aren't just good for you, containing significant amounts of potassium, which is vital for the proper functioning of the nervous system, amongst other things. They're also delicious, filling and their rich, fudgy texture and natural sweetness effectively satisfy cravings for much more sinful treats like chocolate and other sugar laden, calorific delights. Ginger is included to prevent wind building up in your stomach as sweet potatoes are believed to be "windy" or "gassy". A dessert even your grandmother would approve!

6 SMALL TO MEDIUM-SIZED SWEET POTATOES (ABOUT 500 G), SCRUBBED CLEAN, SKIN PEELED AND THICKLY SLICED

1 LARGE PIECE GINGER, SKIN SCRAPED OFF THEN BASHED

3 FRESH OR FROZEN PANDAN LEAVES, WASHED AND KNOTTED

ENOUGH WATER TO COVER SWEET POTATOES

60 G (½ CUP) SOFT BROWN SUGAR OR WHITE SUGAR

1. Combine the sweet potato slices in a pot with ginger, pandan and water and bring to a boil.

2. Lower the heat and simmer until the potato slices are tender right through but still in whole pieces.

3. Sweeten to taste, ensuring all of the sugar dissolves.

4. Turn off the heat and serve in bowls with some of the syrup.

5. If you prefer this cold, cool off, then refrigerate before serving

Pandan leaves, simmered with the rest of the ingredients, lend a gorgeous fragrance to this simple dessert. If these are not available, substitute with 1 teaspoon vanilla extract or ½ teaspoon pandan essence at the end of the cooking time.

Peeled sweet potatoes darken very, very quickly. Once peeled, cover completely with water as you keep peeling the rest. Add the slices to the cooking pot (already filled with water) as you cut each potato. Don't wait until you have sliced all the potatoes before adding to the water in the pot. They would all have blackened by then.

COCONUT CANDY

Prep 15 minutes | Cook 25 minutes | Makes 16 larger or 25 stamp sized pieces

Most versions of coconut candy in Singapore use fresh grated coconut, but as fresh grated coconut is indecently expensive in most parts of the West, compared to what it costs back home, I devised this recipe which uses dessicated coconut. It's much cheaper, and much easier to come by besides. A little more milk, a little less coconut and no one is any the wiser. Shhhh!

SUFFICIENT BUTTER TO GREASE TRAY OR DISH

300 G (2 CUPS) COARSE GRANULATED SUGAR

500 ML (2 ½ CUPS) EVAPORATED MILK

100 G (1 ⅔ CUPS) DESICCATED COCONUT

½ TSP SALT

2 TSP VANILLA EXTRACT

A FEW DROPS FOOD COLOUR OF YOUR CHOICE

1. Grease a 16 cm by 16 cm shallow tray or cake tin with the butter. Combine the sugar and milk in a pot and boil over moderate heat until the sugar completely dissolves and the mixture thickens slightly.

2. Add the coconut and salt and continue to cook, stirring constantly until the mixture thickens, pulls away from the sides of the pan and starts to clump together. Ensure that the mixture doesn't burn. Don't cook until it's too dry or the mixture won't hold together once moulded and cut.

3. Turn off the heat and add the vanilla extract and food colouring. Stir in thoroughly and spread the warm mixture in the greased tray or tin. Press down firmly with the back of a large spoon or with a gloved hand to get an even layer.

4. Cut into pieces with a buttered knife and leave to harden before removing from tray. Keep leftovers in an airtight container and consume within a week. If refrigerated, consume within 3 weeks.

5. If you prefer to have a mixture of colours, divide the warm mixture amongst several containers and colour each differently according to your whim. Proceed to mould the mixture according to the recipe.

WHEN YOU'RE NOT WELL

BRAISED PEANUT AND PORK CONGEE

DILL SEED AND GINGER TEA

CANE SUGAR DRINK

COLD, FEVER AND FLU TEA

PEAR AND HONEY DRINK

POMEGRANATE TEA

BARLEY WATER

BOILED COCA-COLA WITH GINGER AND LEMON

It's often been said that food is medicine. I wouldn't go quite so far, but I think that eating certainly has an effect on your well being. As long as illness has existed, someone somewhere has claimed to have the cure. While I would say "go see a doctor" in most cases, the soothing and relieving effect of some foods cannot be denied. Most of the recipes that follow have been used in my family, in times of illness or poor health, for generations. A few I stumbled upon while satisfying my ever present curiosity. All have been tried and tested and will do you no further harm, but will definitely comfort and soothe, as an adjunct to proper medical care. Yes, what I'm trying to say is, I'm not a doctor and the following recipes are not intended as a replacement for medical treatment, so I am not liable!

BRAISED PEANUT AND PORK CONGEE

Prep 10 mins | Cook 6 hrs | Serves 2

It can be exhilarating and liberating to be away from family and from the watchful eyes of parents, but, you have to admit, there are times when mum's tender loving care is what you long for most. When illness strikes, and she's not there to sponge your brow, make restoring soups or ensure you take your meds, take out your slow cooker, fill it, turn it on then go to bed. When you awake, a bowl of warm comfort almost as good as mum's loving ministrations awaits.

½ CUP JASMINE RICE, WASHED AND DRAINED

800 ML (4 CUPS) WATER

300 G LEAN PORK OR CHICKEN, THINLY SLICED

4 SLICES GINGER, PEELED

1 CAN SOY SAUCE BRAISED PEANUTS,
    BRAISING LIQUID DISCARDED (OR INCLUDE
    IF YOU PREFER)

2 TSP SALT

½ TSP PEPPER

1. Combine all ingredients in a slow cooker and stir well.

2. Turn on "Low" and cover the pot, leaving a slight gap to prevent overboiling and spilling.

3. Leave to cook gently for 6 hours, stirring occasionally to prevent sticking.

4. Ladle out into bowls and serve.

Garnish congee with sesame oil, sliced spring onions and crisp shallots or chilli garlic oil (page 72) for better flavour and presentation.

If you don't have a slow cooker, you can cook this in a securely covered, heavy based, tall and narrow pot placed on an electric hot plate set to minimum heat. Turn off heat after 3 hours and leave covered and undisturbed, until ready to eat.

Drink lots of liquids, get lots of sleep and don't forget to take your meds.

DILL SEED AND GINGER TEA

Prep 5 mins | Cook 15 mins | Makes 4 cups

Stress can sometimes leave your stomach tied up in agonising knots. Few things are more trying than having to slog through your day when all you want to do is curl up on your side until the pain goes away. This simple infusion is one of the most effective remedies I know of to relax a distressed stomach and at the same time it's surprisingly delicious for a curative. My grandmother taught my mother how to make this, and mum in turn taught me; doesn't knowing that already make you feel better?

1 VERY LARGE PIECE GINGER, WASHED, SKIN
    LEFT ON AND BASHED UNTIL SPLIT
A GENEROUS TBSP DILL SEED, CRUSHED WITH
    THE BACK OF A SPOON
4 SMALL LUMPS ROCK SUGAR OR 2 TBSP LIGHT
    BROWN SUGAR
800 ML (4 CUPS) WATER

1. Combine all ingredients in a small pot and bring to a boil.

2. Bring the heat down to minimum, cover pot and simmer very gently for 10 minutes.

3. Turn the heat off and allow solids to settle to the bottom before pouring out the liquid to drink.

4. Sip continuously whilst very warm. Drink 1 cup every 3−4 hours. Your pain should be much reduced after the second cup.

If dill seeds are unavailable, use fennel seeds which are very nearly as effective and much easier to find.

This infusion is also very helpful for menstrual pain and discomforts.

If pain and symptoms persist after 24 hours, seek medical attention.

If it's not life and death and it doesn't impact your future, don't sweat it! Chill and remember, things are always better after a nap.

CANE SUGAR DRINK (FOR HIVES AND SKIN RASHES)

Prep 5 mins | Serves 1

When I was a child, I lived next door to the neighbourhood Chinese medicine woman, with whom my grandmother became very chummy, and from whom she wheedled out countless home remedies, including this one, in exchange for treasured recipes. Knowing how guarded my grandmother was about her recipes, I can only hope that the medicine woman did not have a similar affliction. I did break out in hives once, and while I can't decide if this helped, I know it didn't harm. My advice would be, see a doctor and brew this pleasant drink to distract yourself from the itchies and the aches.

1 WALNUT-SIZED LUMP GOLDEN ROCK SUGAR
VERY HOT BOILED WATER

1. Break up the sugar and put into a mug.

2. Pour over the hot water and stir to dissolve sugar.

3. Sip while still warm.

4. Repeat every 3 hours until you feel relief.

> Golden rock sugar looks like regular rock sugar except it has a light amber colour, the result of being boiled down from sugar cane juice. It is believed to be more cooling than regular rock sugar. You should be able to find it in your neighbourhood Asian grocer. I don't know if regular rock sugar will work here. But you could give it a try if you can't find the golden variety.

COLD, FEVER AND FLU TEA

Prep 5 mins | Serves 1

This is my boy's remedy for influenza and the common cold. It tastes pleasant enough, so far as "medicinal" concoctions go. And it works pretty damned well too. I can't remember the last time he's been to the doctor for coughs, colds or the flu. By no means am I saying that this is a cure-all. If you are really ill, please go see a doctor. This will get you through minor sniffles or tide you over until you can get proper medical attention.

1 SACHET COLD OR FLU REMEDY POWDER,
  LIKE LEMSIP OR PANADOL COLD AND
  FLU REMEDY
1 CUP VERY HOT WATER
1 BLACK OR GREEN TEA BAG (GREEN TEA IS
  SAID TO HAVE MORE BUG ZAPPING POWER)
JUICE OF HALF A SMALL LEMON
3 TSP HONEY

1. Tear the sachet of cold remedy powder and pour out the contents into a large cup or mug.

2. Pour the water into a cup and stir until the powder dissolves. Pop in a teabag and steep for about 3–5 minutes before discarding teabag.

3. Add the lemon juice and honey, stir, then taste and add more honey if necessary.

4. Sip while still hot and get plenty of rest. Repeat every 4–6 hours until you feel better.

If you're having stomach flu and feel nauseated on top of everything else, add 3 large slices of peeled and bashed fresh ginger to the flu powder, before pouring in hot water. Proceed according to the recipe, except don't discard the ginger. Re-use the ginger twice more before discarding and replacing with fresh ginger.

PEAR AND HONEY DRINK (FOR DRY COUGH)

Prep 10 mins | Cook 1 hr | Makes 4 cups

This is something my grandmother often made for me as I used to get a scratchy, irritated throat and dry cough very often. It's also very pleasant tasting and refreshing when chilled but it should be sipped warm for best results.

2 LARGE, UNBLEMISHED CHINESE PEARS, STEMS, SEEDS AND CORE DISCARDED, THEN WASHED AND QUARTERED

1 L (5 CUPS) WATER

4 TBSP CHINESE WINTER HONEY OR ANY MILD TASTING HONEY

1. Combine everything in a steel or enamel pot (do not use aluminium or iron pots).

2. Bring to a boil, then reduce heat and simmer for 45 minutes or until the pears are tender.

3. Turn off the heat and pour out the liquid. Sip while warm.

If your throat still hurts, make another batch with fresh pears. If it really, really hurts, go see a doctor.

Chill the pears and eat once your throat feels better. My grandmother never let me eat the pears but never offered any explanation; they were always discarded. I eat them now simply because I can't bear to throw out food.

POMEGRANATE TEA (FOR DIARRHOEA)

Prep 2 mins | Serves 1

If you like pomegranates (I find eating them quite entertaining) save the peel next time you eat one… or three. Pomegranate peels are believed to be especially high in tannic acids which are very helpful when you're suffering from umm… you know, the "D" word. After you've eaten the "seeds", dry the peels by wiping them, then leave them on a clean cloth by a sunny window or next to your radiator until they shrivel and turn brown and papery. Store in a clean air tight container until you need them.

A GENEROUS TBSP POMEGRANATE PEEL
(TAKE A LARGE PIECE AND BREAK INTO
ENOUGH SMALL PIECES TO FILL A SPOON)
1 COFFEE MUG OF FRESHLY BOILED WATER

1. Put the peel into a coffee mug and pour over very hot water.

2. Cover the mug and leave to steep until the water cools to warm.

3. Drink half the liquid, then drink the remaining half 3–4 hours later.

4. Steep the peel with freshly boiled water again and drink.

You can also make this tea with fresh peels but use 3 times as much fresh as dry peel.

When you have diarrhoea, don't eat anything fibrous, fatty, oily, milky, coconutty or spicy. Stick to food like dry toast, fat-free plain crackers, plain rice porridge with soy sauce or things like Marmite and Bovril diluted in hot water. Black tea, unsweetened, is also good but not coffee, which has a laxative effect. Also avoid honey.

BARLEY WATER

Prep 10 mins | Cook 35 mins | Makes about 700 ml

When I was a child, and medical doctors didn't inspire as much confidence as they do today, barley water was a wondrous remedy for painfully raw throats and defiant fevers that didn't respond to medications. Of course you should consult a doctor if your fever stubbornly rages on. Even so, this fragrant and refreshing drink is a lovely adjunct to proper medical care.

150 G (1 CUP) PEARL BARLEY

4 FRESH OR FROZEN PANDAN LEAVES, WASHED
    AND KNOTTED

1.4 L (7 CUPS) WATER

4 WALNUT-SIZED LUMPS (ABOUT 100G)
    ROCK SUGAR OR ⅔ CUP REGULAR SUGAR

1. Remove any impurities from the barley and rinse 2 or 3 times.

2. Drain and put into a kettle or pot with all other ingredients, except rock sugar.

3. Bring to a boil over medium heat and turn the heat down to a simmer.

4. Cook gently (cover partially if using a pot) for about 20 minutes or until the barley just expands.

5. Add the rock sugar, simmer briefly just until the sugar dissolves, then turn off heat.

6. Stir, then allow to settle for a few minutes before pouring out the liquid.

7. Drink warm or hot, every few hours.

Once all the liquid is drunk and the barley seeds are still fresh and edible and can be reused once more, add more water to the barley and repeat the process again according to the recipe. Finish the resulting liquid, then discard the barley.

BOILED COCA-COLA WITH GINGER AND LEMON

Prep 5 mins | Cook 10 mins | Serves 1

This supposedly tried and true, "ancient" Chinese remedy, is more precisely said to originate from Hong Kong. It really does dull the pain of a raw throat, though you have to wonder, just how ancient Coca-Cola is. As with gift horses, folk remedies usually don't stand up to close scrutiny, but anything that provides comfort and tastes pleasant enough shouldn't be dismissed so quickly. So, the next time your throat feels like it's been rasped by sandpaper, give this a try. A gravel ground voice may sound sexy, but it certainly doesn't feel anywhere near as good.

5 CM GINGER

½ MEDIUM-SIZED LEMON, THINLY SLICED

1 CAN COCA-COLA (STILL FIZZY)

EXTRA LEMON SLICES, TO GARNISH
   (OPTIONAL—BUT CHEERFUL AND
   RECOMMENDED FOR LOW SPIRITS)

1. Put the ginger and lemon slices into a non-reactive pot.

2. Pour the Coca-Cola into the pot and bring to a boil. Lower the heat and simmer for 5–10 minutes, depending on how "potent" you want it.

3. Turn off the heat and allow to cool slightly. Put the extra lemon slices into a mug or heatproof glass. Strain the drink into the mug and sip while still hot.

"Non-reactive" refers to materials that don't react to acid substances. Examples are stainless steel, glass, ceramic and glazed clay or earthernware. Examples of reactive materials are aluminium, cast iron, copper and some plastics which can be "eaten" or leached (reactions) by acids and leak undesirable chemical substances into any acidic (like lemon juice or vinegar) liquids they are in contact with, especially when these liquids are heated.

This drink increases in both potency (effectiveness) and flavour intensity the longer you simmer it. If you prefer a milder flavour, simmer it for the shorter recommended time and vice versa.

This drink is said to have diminished "potency" when it cools.

CONVERSION TABLES

Amounts are approximate and rounded up or down for convenience. For best results, stick to one system of measurement, e.g., either completely Metric, Imperial or American. Do not mix measurements systems, especially when baking, or you may not get the desired results.

TEMPERATURE

OVEN DESCRIPTION	GAS MARK	TEMP. °C	TEMP. °F
Cool	1	140°C	280°F
	2	150°C	300°F
Warm	3	160°C	320°F
Moderate	4	180°C	350°F
Moderately Hot	5	190°C	370°F
	6	200°C	390°F
Hot	7	210°C	410°F
	8	220°C	430°F
Very Hot	9	230°C	445°F
		240°C	465°F
		250°C	480°F

WEIGHTS AND MEASURES

AMOUNT	GRAMS	MILLILITRES	OUNCES	POUNDS	SPOONS
1 teaspoon	6 g	5 ml			
1 tablespoon	18 g	15 ml			3 tsp
1 cup	100 g	200 ml	3.5 oz 7 fl oz		13 tbsp
1 kilogram	1000 g			2 lb 4 oz	
1 pound	454 g		16 oz		
1 ounce	28 g	25 ml			1½ tbsp
1 litre		1000 ml	36 fl oz		

CUP MEASUREMENT

1 STANDARD TEA CUP	GRAMS	MILLILITRES	OUNCES
Flour	100 g		3.5 oz
Butter	150 g		5.3 oz
White Sugar	150 g		5.3 oz
Brown Sugar	120 g		4.2 oz
Icing (confectioner's) Sugar	90 g		3.2 oz
Cocoa Powder	90 g		3.2 oz
Liquids and Oils	100 g (usually)	200 ml	3.5 oz 7 fl oz
Dessicated Coconut	60 g		2.1 oz
Chopped Nuts	120 g		4.2 oz
Finely Ground Nuts (nut meal)	100 g		3.5 oz
Mini Chocolate Chips	120 g		4.2 oz
Uncooked Rice	150 g		5.3 oz
Light Cereals and Grains (oats, wheat, etc.)	100 g		3.5 oz

G gram • **KG** kilogram • **ML** millilitre • **L** litre • **OZ** ounce • **FL OZ** fluid ounce
LB pound • **TSP** teaspoon • **TBSP** tablespoon

INDEX

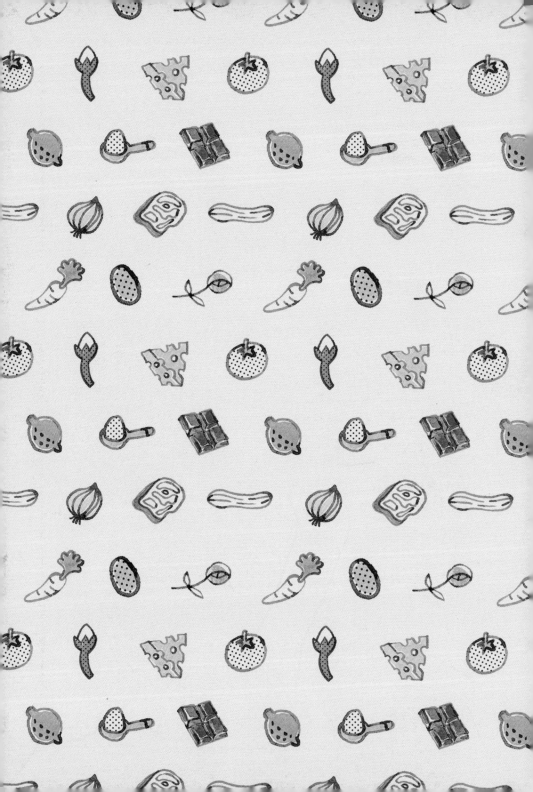